Introduction

This book supports children preparing for the 11+ entrance exam. The the book are carefully modelled after past papers to ensure that the provide a rich and varied practice to meet all requirements of 1 appropriate difficulty.

Papers are designed to teach students the most easily applicable, reusable and fastest solutions to typical problems, and utilise problems which target areas of maths that children typically forget under the pressure of an exam. Solutions provided have been reviewed by many children to ensure that they are easily understandable while being the fastest and most re-applicable.

Each practice paper becomes progressively more complex as you work through the paper. They require the basic knowledge of arithmetical operations of addition, subtraction, multiplication and division, simple algebra, up to level 5 of the National Curriculum (Key Stage 2). Most questions involve straightforward mathematical calculations. Some questions are designed to test a child's ability to extract the necessary information to solve a mathematical problem from questions worded in English. The paper is designed not only for children to prepare for admission exams but also for those aiming for scholarship.

After completing these practice papers, you should be able to:
1. Quickly formulate optimal solutions to any 11+ maths question.
2. More readily apply previously learnt skills on a question to question basis.

11+ Maths Practice Papers comprises of 2 books. Each book contains 4 full practice papers, while each practice paper contains 30 questions and solutions.

Contents

1	Paper 1	1
2	Paper 2	16
3	Paper 3	32
4	Paper 4	48
5	Paper 1 solutions	61
6	Paper 2 solutions	75
7	Paper 3 solutions	92
8	Paper 4 solutions	106

Paper 1

Materials
For this paper you must have:
- Pen, pencil, eraser and ruler.

Time allowed
1 hour.

Instructions
- Aim to complete as much as you can in the time given, without making mistakes.
- You must answer the questions in the space provided.
- Show all your working. You may be awarded marks for correct working even if your final answer is incorrect, and a correct answer unsupported by correct working may not receive full marks.
- Diagrams are not accurately drawn, unless otherwise indicated.
- Calculators are **NOT** allowed.

Information
- There are 30 questions on this paper
- The marks for questions are shown in brackets.
- The maximum mark is 100.

Advice
- Read each question carefully before you start to answer it.
- Keep an eye on the time.
- Don't worry if you don't complete the paper. If you get stuck, just go on to the next question and if you have time at the end come back to the one(s) you left.

1(a) 9999 + 777 + 33 + 1

Answer... 1800 ... (1 mark)

1(b) 437 − 229

$$\begin{array}{r} 4\overset{2}{\cancel{3}}\overset{1}{7} \\ -\ 229 \\ \hline 208 \end{array}$$

Answer... 208 ... (1 mark)

2(a) 99 × 38

3762

Answer... 3762 ... (1 mark)

2(b) 71.1 ÷ 9

$$9\overline{)\underset{63}{71.1}}07.9$$
$$81$$

Answer... 7.9 ... (1 mark)

3(a) $\frac{5}{8} + \frac{3}{16}$

Answer... 13/16 ... (1 mark)

3(b) $1\frac{1}{4} - \frac{3}{8}$

7

Answer......$\frac{7}{8}$...... (2 marks)

4(a) What number must be added to 59 to give the result 3100?

Answer......3041...... (2 marks)

4(b) Write down any fraction between $\frac{1}{3}$ and $\frac{1}{2}$.

Answer..........1/4.................. (2 marks)

5(a) Work out $(58+57+56+55) - (57+56+55+54)$

  2 26   2 22

4

Answer........4.......... (2 marks)

5(b) What is the greatest whole number that you can make using the digits 5, 4, 9 and 8? Use each digit only once.

98

Answer....9854.......... (2 marks)

10

6(a) What is 25% of 40?

....

Answer.......... 10 .... (2 marks)

6(b) What is 40% of 25?

....

Answer.......... 10 .... (2 marks)

6(c) What is 50% of 25% of 40?

....

Answer.......... 5 .... (2 marks)

7 Arrange the digits 7, 6, 5, and 4 so that the resulting number is closest to five thousand.

....

Answer...... 4765 .... (2 marks)

8 Write the correct number in each box.

$$\frac{3}{5} = \frac{\boxed{9}}{15} = \frac{12}{\boxed{20}} = \frac{\boxed{15}}{25} = \frac{27}{\boxed{40}}$$ (2 marks)

....

10

9 Circle the two numbers from the list below which have a total of 0.15

0.1   (0.09)   0.5   0.14   (0.06)   (2 marks)

10 Write the correct number in each box.

10(a) 200 = 40 ÷ [8500]   200   (2 marks)

10(b) $\frac{63.2}{[10]} = 632$ (2 marks)

10(c) 73.5 × [0.5] = 7.35   (2 marks)

10(d) 100 = 35 ÷ [350]   (2 marks)

35 ÷ □ = 100   10 ÷ □ = 5
                  10 ÷ 5 = □
35 ÷ 100 = 0.35

11 Emma has four number cards:

| 1 | 2 | 8 | 9 |

She arranges them to form two 2 digit numbers. She multiplies the numbers together. Which two 2 digit numbers give the largest answer?

Answer... 98 × 21   (2 marks)

12(a) $2 - 1\frac{7}{11}$

$\frac{4}{11}$ ✓

Answer............   (2 marks)

12(b) $\frac{1}{5} + \frac{2}{15}$

Answer... $\frac{5}{15}$ or $\frac{1}{3}$ (2 marks)

13 Shortcrust pastry is made using flour and fat in the ratio 2:1.
How many grams of flour are needed to make 450 grams of shortcrust pastry?

    150
  3)450   150×2=300   2+1=3
                            450÷3=

Answer... 300g   (2 marks)

8

14(a) Find the area of the rectangle shown below.

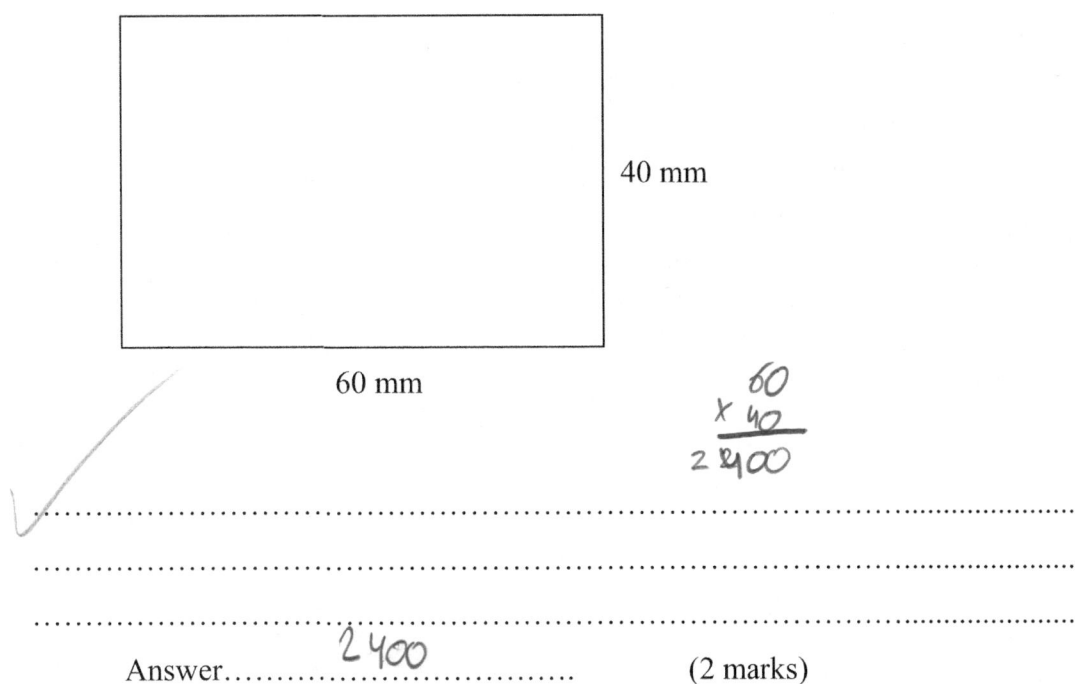

60 mm

60
× 40
2400 [shown as "2 8400" with crossed digit]

Answer......2400...... (2 marks)

14(b) Jack cuts the rectangle up into an exact number of right-angled triangles, each with sides as shown in the diagram below.

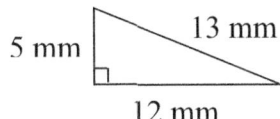

Calculate the number of triangles that he can cut from the rectangle.

Answer......2...... (2 marks)

14(c) What fraction of the figure is shaded?

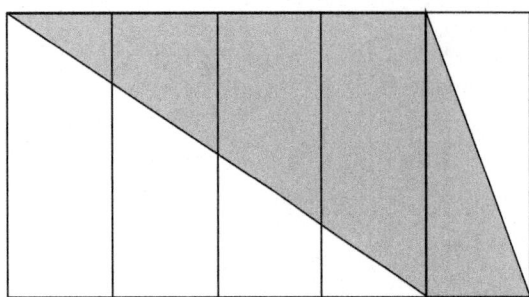

....
....
....
Answer.............$\frac{1}{2}$............. (2 marks)

15 Find the size of angle 'a' in the diagram below.

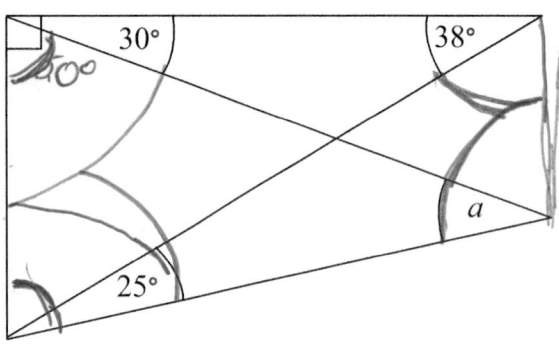

....
....
....
....
....
....
Answer............25............. (2 marks)

16(a) Emma takes 38 minutes to travel to work each morning. She leaves home at 8.15 a.m. What time does she arrive at work?

Answer......8:53............ (2 marks)

16(b) The journey home in the evening takes the same time. She arrives home at 6.24 p.m. At what time did she leave work?

6:00 − 14 min = 5:46

Answer........5.............. (2 marks)

17 My age is a multiple of 9. Next year it will be a multiple of 5. I am more than 30 years old, but less than 80. How old am I?

Answer........54............ (2 marks)

18 $805 = a \times b \times c$, where a, b and c are prime numbers, with c is bigger than b, and b bigger than a.

Find a, b and c

Answer............... (3 marks)

19 The figure below is made up of ten equal squares. The perimeter of the figure is 112 cm.

What is the area of one of the squares?

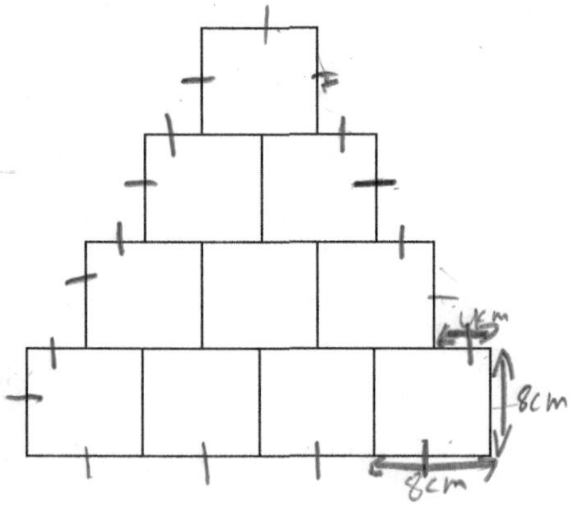

Answer............64cm............ (3 marks)

20 A bus has 35 passengers on board. At the first stop two fifths get off and then 7 people get on. At the next stop a quarter of the people remaining on the bus get off and then 13 get on.

How many passengers are there on the bus now?

$\frac{1}{5}$ of 35 = 7   35 − 14 + 7 = 28

$\frac{1}{4}$ of 28 = 7 + 13 = 20

Answer............20............ (3 marks)

21(a) Find two numbers which when multiplied together make a hundred. Neither of the two numbers must use any 0s.

4 × 25

Answer............4 × 25............ (2 marks)

21(b) Find two numbers which when multiplied together make a thousand. Once again, neither of the two numbers must use any 0s.

Answer... 125 × 8 .... (2 marks)

22(a) I turn 50 degrees clockwise, 80 degrees anticlockwise and finally 90 degrees clockwise. If I want to return to my original position by turning through the smallest possible angle, in which direction should I turn and what should the angle be?

Answer...... 60° anticlockwise (2 marks)

22(b) If I face West and turn 270 degrees clockwise, in which direction am I now facing?

Answer............ South ...... (2 marks)

23 In the boxes, write the numbers that their arrows are pointing to.

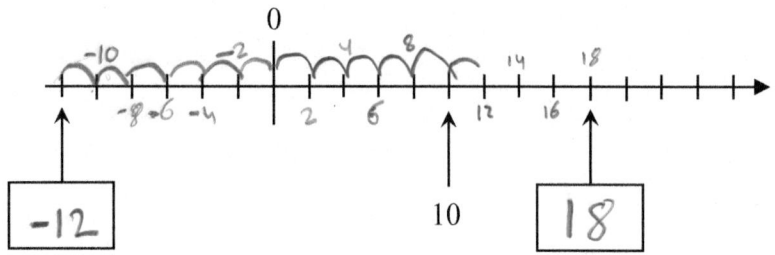

−12   10   18

(2 marks)

24 Look at the number pattern below:

$1^2 + 3 = 4$

$2^2 + 5 = 9$

$3^2 + 7 = 16$

24(a) Fill in the next two lines of the pattern,

$\underline{4^2} + \underline{9} = \underline{25}$

$\underline{5^2} + \underline{11} = \underline{36}$

(2 marks)

$6^2 + 13 = 49$
$7^2 + 15 = 64$
$8^2 + 17 = 81$
$9^2 + 19 = 100$
$10^2 + 21 = 121$

24(b) Complete the following line which comes later in the pattern.

$\underline{11^2} + \underline{23} = 144$

(2 marks)

25   *ABCD* is a rectangle. What is the area of the shaded region?

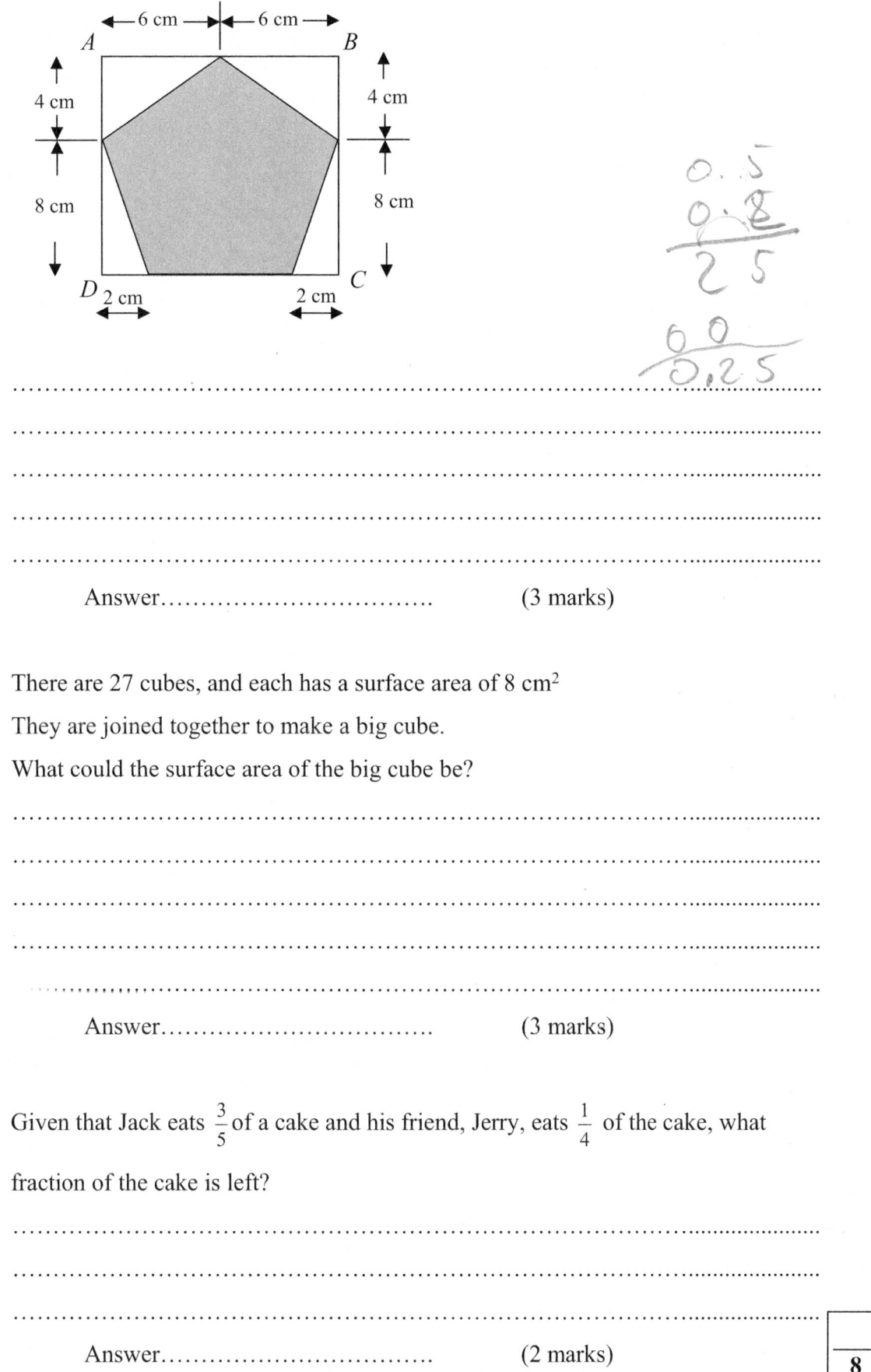

....
....
....
....
....

Answer................................   (3 marks)

26   There are 27 cubes, and each has a surface area of 8 cm²

They are joined together to make a big cube.

What could the surface area of the big cube be?

....
....
....
....
....

Answer................................   (3 marks)

27(a)   Given that Jack eats $\frac{3}{5}$ of a cake and his friend, Jerry, eats $\frac{1}{4}$ of the cake, what fraction of the cake is left?

....
....
....

Answer................................   (2 marks)

27(b) Given that Jack's piece of cake weighed 150 grams, what was the weight of the whole cake?

....
....
....
....

Answer……………………….   (2 marks)

27(c) Jack uses 650 g of sugar from a 3.5 kg packet. How many kilograms of sugar are left?

....
....
....
....

Answer……………………….   (2 marks)

28   25 students have taken an exam and the mean number of marks is recorded as 82. The examiner subsequently awards 5 additional marks to 9 of the students and takes away 3 marks from 10 other students.
What will the new mean mark be?

....
....
....
....
....
....

Answer……………………….   (2 marks)

29 I am thinking of a number less than 60.

When my number is divided by 4, it gives remainder 2.

When my number is divided by 5, it gives remainder 3.

When my number is divided by 6, it gives remainder 4.

What number am I thinking of?

....

....

....

....

....

....

Answer................................ (3 marks)

30 A car leaves Birmingham New Street travelling 50 miles per hour. An hour later, a second car leaves Birmingham New Street following the first car, travelling 70 miles per hour.

How long will it take the second car to overtake the first car, after leaving Birmingham New Street?

....

....

....

....

....

....

Answer................................ (3 marks)

Paper 2

Materials

For this paper you must have:
- Pen, pencil, eraser and ruler.

Time allowed

1 hour.

Instructions
- Aim to complete as much as you can in the time given, without making mistakes.
- You must answer the questions in the space provided.
- Show all your working. You may be awarded marks for correct working even if your final answer is incorrect, and a correct answer unsupported by correct working may not receive full marks.
- Diagrams are not accurately drawn, unless otherwise indicated.
- Calculators are **NOT** allowed.

Information
- There are 30 questions on this paper
- The marks for questions are shown in brackets.
- The maximum mark is 100.

Advice
- Read each question carefully before you start to answer it.
- Keep an eye on the time.
- Don't worry if you don't complete the paper. If you get stuck, just go on to the next question and if you have time at the end come back to the one(s) you left.

1(a)　What number is 1000 more than 45678?

....
....
....

　　　　　　Answer……………………………　(1 mark)

1(b)　What number is 0·02 more than 14·99?

....
....
....

　　　　　　Answer……………………………　(1 mark)

2(a)
```
    8 8 8 8
      7 7 7
  +     3 3
          2
  ─────────

  ─────────
```

　　　　　　Answer……………………………　(2 marks)

2(b)
```
    5 4 3 2 1
  - 1 2 3 4 5
  ───────────

  ───────────
```

　　　　　　Answer……………………………　(2 marks)

3(a)　596 × 35

....
....
....
....

　　　　　　Answer……………………………　(2 marks)

8

3(b) $2024 \div 8$

....
....
....
....
....
....

             Answer............................   (2 marks)

4   What is half of $45\frac{1}{2}$?

....
....
....

             Answer............................   (2 marks)

5(a)   4444 p   =   £............................ (2 marks)

....
....

5(b)   40 cm   = ...m   (2 marks)

....
....

5(c)   1 m 5 cm   = ...m   (2 marks)

....
....

5(d)   3 m 50 cm   = ...cm   (2 marks)

....
....

12

5(e) $3\frac{1}{3}$ hr   =   ………………minutes   (2 marks)

....

....

6   Arrange the following decimals from the smallest to the largest

     1.4   1.42   1.04   1.402   (2 marks)

....

....

7   Jack is three times as heavy as Emma. If Jack is 8 kg heavier than Emma. What is the weight of Jack in kg?

....

....

....

....

....

....

         Answer…………………………….   (2 marks)

8   A carpet which measures 6 m × 4 m covers 60% of the floor area of a rectangular room. The length of the room is 8 m. What is its width?

....

....

....

....

....

....

         Answer…………………………….   (2 marks)

9   A mosaic pattern is arranged as shown using balls.

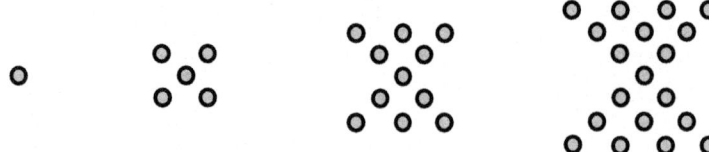

Any number in this sequence can be found as follows:

1st Pattern $(1 \times 2) - 1 = 1$

2nd Pattern $(2 \times 3) - 1 = 5$

3rd Pattern $(3 \times 4) - 1 = 11$

9(a) Fill in the next two lines of the pattern,

____ - ____ = ____   (1 mark)

____ - ____ = ____   (1 mark)

9(b) Complete the following line which comes later in the pattern.

____ - ____ = 109   (2 marks)

10 Write the following events in order, with the most probable (i.e. most likely) first and the least probable (i.e. least likely) last. Give your answer as a sequence of letters, e.g. BACED.

A: Being born on the weekend;

B: Being born on Christmas Eve;

C: Rolling a 4 with a fair cube die;

D: Obtaining a head when a fair coin is tossed;

E: Obtaining an even number when two odd numbers are multiplied together.

Answer............................... (3 marks)

11 Complete the train time table below.

Route	Departs	Arrives	Journey Time
London – Birmingham	09:45		1 hr 20 min
London – Manchester	11:05	13:03	
London – Carlisle		16:12	3 hr 17 min

(3 marks)

12 A wire costs £1.02 per metre.

12(a) How much will it cost to buy 10 metres?

Answer................................ (2 marks)

12(b) Jack buys a length of wire costing £25.50. How many metres does he buy?

Answer................................ (2 marks)

13 Five miles is the same distance as eight kilometres. Use this fact to convert 120 kilometres into miles.

Answer................................ (2 marks)

14   There are 68 apples in a box. 25% of them are red and the rest are green. How many green apples are there in the box?

   ....
   ....
   ....

   Answer……………………….   (2 marks)

15   Here are three lamps.
   Lamp A flashes every 4 minutes. Lamp B flashes every 6 minutes. Lamp C flashes every 8 minutes. The three lamps start flashing at 10.00 a. m., at what time will they next flash together?

   ....
   ....
   ....
   ....
   ....
   ....

   Answer……………………….   (2 marks)

16   Cans are often stacked like this in a supermarket display.

   Row 1
   Row 2
   Row 3
   Row 4

16(a)   Find the total number of cans in the first four rows.

   ....
   ....
   ....
   ....

   Answer……………………….   (2 marks)

16(b) How many rows would be needed to display 36 cans?

....
....
....
....

       Answer…………………………….   (2 marks)

17   A cube with sides 4 cm is made from smaller cubes of side 1cm as shown.

17(a) How many small cubes are used in making the bigger cube?

....
....
....

       Answer…………………………….   (2 marks)

17(b) If the bigger cube is painted red all over, how many small cubes will have one red face?

....
....
....
....

       Answer…………………………….   (2 marks)

17(c) How many small cubes will have 2 red faces?

....

....

....

....

Answer……………………….   (2 marks)

18   A large rectangle is made by joining five identical small rectangles as shown.

Diagram **NOT** accurately drawn

The perimeter of one small rectangle is 50 cm.

Work out the perimeter of the large rectangle.

....

....

....

....

....

....

....

....

Answer……………………….   (2 marks)

19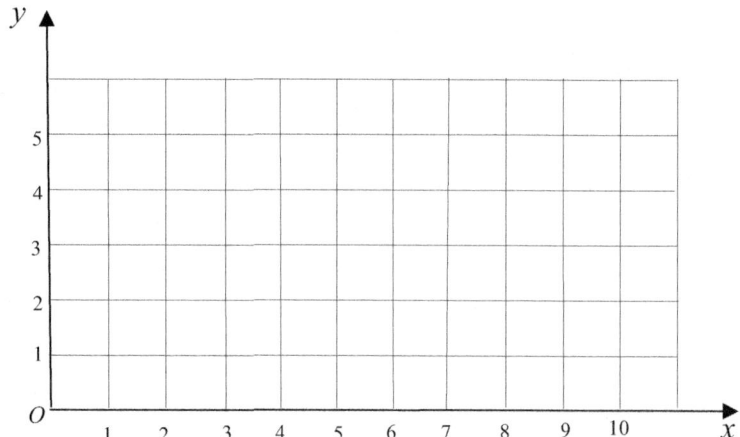

19(a) On the grid above, plot and label the points *A* (2, 3) , *B*(4, 5) , *C* (8, 3) and *D* (4,1) .
(2 marks)

....
....
....

19(b) Join *ABCD*. (1 mark)

....
....

19(c) What name is given to this shape?

Answer……………………………. (2 marks)

19(d) Find the coordinates of the point of intersection of the diagonals.

....
....
....
....

Answer……………………………. (2 marks)

19(e) Draw on any lines of symmetry. (1 mark)

....
....

19(f) Calculate the area of *ABCD*.

....

....

....

Answer.............................. (2 marks)

20 This factory was built in the year in which Jack was born. Jack was 30 years old in the 1995. How old was this factory in 2018?

....

....

....

Answer.............................. (2 marks)

21 Along any line drawn, the numbers in the two circles at the end of a line should multiply to make the number in the square between the two circles.

Fill the remaining squares and circles with numbers obeying this rule.

(2 marks)

....

....

....

....

....

22 In a children's game you call out all the numbers from 1 to 100. You clap every time you say either a multiple of 7 or a number ending in 7. How many times would you clap?

   ....
   ....
   ....
   ....
   ....
   ....

   Answer................................ (2 marks)

23 In a box of pens, one third are black, one fifth are red and the rest are blue. What fraction of the pens is blue?

   ....
   ....
   ....

   Answer................................ (2 marks)

24 To cook a joint of beef, you leave it in the oven for 30 minutes for every kilogram it weighs, plus 20 minutes extra. Find how long you would cook a joint weighing:

24(a) 2 kg

   ....
   ....
   ....

   Answer................................ (2 marks)

24(b) 3.5 kg

   ....
   ....
   ....

   Answer................................ (2 marks)

25   Six football teams play each other once. How many matches will need to be played?

....

Answer.............................. (3 marks)

26   Write down (in simplest form) the fraction that the arrow is pointing to.

$$\frac{1}{5} \quad \frac{3}{10} \quad \uparrow \quad \frac{1}{2}$$

....

Answer.............................. (2 marks)

27   When two numbers are added together, the result is 32. When the smaller number is subtracted from the larger one, the result is 6. Find these two numbers.

....

Answer.............................. (2 marks)

28(a) Yesterday's tomorrow is Friday.

What day is the day after tomorrow's yesterday?

Answer.............................. (2 marks)

28(b) If March 23rd is a Monday, on what day of the week is April 2nd?

Answer.............................. (2 marks)

29   Write the correct digit in each box.

(a)

```
    1  5  □  9
 +     □  7  □
 ─────────────
    2  4  4  3
```

(2 marks)

29(b)

```
       □  6  3
  ×          □
 ─────────────
    3  9  □  1
```

(2 marks)

30   In Miss Fryer's class, there are 5 girls for every 4 boys, and one fifth of the girls wear glasses. There are three girls and two boys in the class who wear glasses. What fraction of all the pupils in the class wear glasses?

....
....
....
....
....
....
....
....
....

Answer................................   (3 marks)

Paper 3

Materials

For this paper you must have:
- Pen, pencil, eraser and ruler.

Time allowed

1 hour.

Instructions
- Aim to complete as much as you can in the time given, without making mistakes.
- You must answer the questions in the space provided.
- Show all your working. You may be awarded marks for correct working even if your final answer is incorrect, and a correct answer unsupported by correct working may not receive full marks.
- Diagrams are not accurately drawn, unless otherwise indicated.
- Calculators are **NOT** allowed.

Information
- There are 30 questions on this paper
- The marks for questions are shown in brackets.
- The maximum mark is 100.

Advice
- Read each question carefully before you start to answer it.
- Keep an eye on the time.
- Don't worry if you don't complete the paper. If you get stuck, just go on to the next question and if you have time at the end come back to the one(s) you left.

1(a) $2\frac{1}{2} + 4\frac{1}{4}$

....
....
....

Answer............................... (1 mark)

1(b) $4\frac{1}{4} - 2\frac{1}{2}$

....
....
....

Answer............................... (1 mark)

2(a) $3\frac{1}{2} \times 1\frac{1}{3}$

....
....
....

Answer............................... (1 mark)

2(b) $10 \div \frac{1}{4}$

....
....
....

Answer............................... (2 marks)

2(c) $\frac{1}{2}$ of $\frac{3}{4}$

....
....
....

Answer............................... (2 marks)

3(a) $\frac{3}{8}$ of 240 m.

....
....
....

Answer................................ (2 marks)

3(b) 20% of £350

....
....
....

Answer................................ (2 marks)

4(a) £1.28+57p

....
....
....

Answer................................ (2 marks)

4(b) £1.28-57p

....
....
....

Answer................................ (2 marks)

5(a) A number is multiplied by 100 to give 2030
What is the number?

....
....
....

Answer................................ (2 marks)

5(b) 7686×5

Answer.............................. (2 marks)

6(a) A Year 6 student sleeps for 9 hours every day. For what fraction of the day, in its simplest form, is the student awake?

Answer.............................. (2 marks)

6(b) What fraction of 2.4 litres is 400 ml?

Answer.............................. (2 marks)

7 Write in figures the number three hundred thousand and thirty.

Answer.............................. (2 marks)

8 Put these numbers in ascending order.

$5^2 \qquad 2^5 \qquad 3^4 \qquad 4^3$

Answer.............................. (2 marks)

9   For a film, the seats cost £3 for each child and £8 for each adult. I was charged £52 for all the seats I bought.

9(a)   Did I buy more than 6 adult tickets?

....

....

....

   Answer……………………………..   (2 marks)

9(b)   If there were more adult tickets than child tickets, how many of each did I buy?

....

....

....

....

....

....

   Answer……………………………..   (2 marks)

9(c)   If there were more child tickets than adult tickets, how many of each did I buy?

....

....

....

....

....

....

   Answer……………………………..   (2 marks)

10   Every day Jack runs 3 km.

10(a)   Find out how far he runs in 4 weeks.

....

....

....

   Answer…………………………….   (2 marks)

10(b) If he takes 15 minutes to run the 3 km, what is the average speed in kilometres per hour?

....
....
....

Answer……………………….   (2 marks)

11   Eggs are sold in boxes of 12, costing £1.68. I wish to make 15 cakes for a local fete. The recipe requires 5 eggs for each cake.

11(a) How many eggs will I use altogether to make 15 cakes?

....
....
....

Answer……………………….   (2 marks)

11(b) How many boxes must I buy to ensure I have enough eggs for the cakes?

....
....
....
....

Answer……………………….   (2 marks)

11(c) How much will I pay for the eggs?

....
....
....
....

Answer……………………….   (2 marks)

12   The exchange rate was £1 = 12 HKD.

12(a)   In Hong Kong, Jack wanted buy a large bar of chocolate, which cost £3.

How much would Jack have to pay for chocolate in HKD?

....

....

....

Answer................................   (2 marks)

12(b)   The price for a watch is 480 HKD.

How much is it in English pounds?

....

....

....

Answer................................   (2 marks)

13   Fill in the two missing numbers in each of following sequences:

13(a)   8, 12, ☐, 20, 24, ☐, 32   (2 marks)

....

....

13(b)   256, 128, 64, ☐, 16, 8, ☐.   (2 marks)

....

....

14   Which of the following is greater than 3 but smaller than 4?

$\frac{10}{3}$ $\frac{12}{3}$ $\frac{9}{3}$ $\frac{8}{3}$

....

....

....

....

Answer................................   (2 marks)

15 A pineapple costs £2.45

Jack has a £10 note.

He buys as many pineapples as he can with his £10 note.

15(a) How many pineapples does Jack buy?

....

....

....

Answer................................ (2 marks)

15(b) How much change should Jack receive from his £10 note?

....

....

....

Answer................................ (2 marks)

16 One of the angles of an isosceles triangle is 96°. Find the sizes of the other two angles.

....

....

....

....

....

....

....

Answer................................ (2 marks)

17(a) Shade in $\frac{2}{5}$ of the shape below.

(2 marks)

....
....
....
....
....

17(b) Shade in 60% of the shape below.

(2 marks)

....
....
....
....
....
....

18 Emma starts with a number, doubles it and then subtracts 9. The result is 33
What number did Emma start with?

....
....
....
....
....

Answer................................ (2 marks)

19 Jane is $10\frac{1}{2}$ years old. Her brother is exactly 1 year and 8 months younger than Jane.

How old is her brother?

....
....
....
....
....
....

Answer................................ (2 marks)

20   Here are the ingredients needed to make 12 muffins.

Ingredients to make 12 muffins
300 g flour
150 g sugar
250 ml milk
100 g butter
2 eggs

20(a) Emma makes 60 muffins.

Work out how much flour she uses.

....

....

....

....

       Answer................................   (2 marks)

20(b) Jack makes some muffins.

He uses 600 g sugar.

Work out how many muffins he makes.

....

....

....

....

....

       Answer................................   (2 marks)

21(a) Which number between 40 and 50 is a multiple of both 4 and 6?

....
....
....
....
....
....

        Answer................................ (2 marks)

21(b) Circle the three numbers in the list below which have a sum of 43.

     5   8   11   14   21   31   (2 marks)

....
....

22 Jack and Emma each think of a number.

The difference between their numbers is 8.

The sum of their numbers is 30.

What are the two numbers?

....
....
....
....
....

        Answer................................ (2 marks)

23 Emma has used her calculator to find out that $14 \times 541 = 7574$

Use Emma's calculator to find out

23(a) 140×541 (1 mark)

....

23(b) 14×540 (1 mark)

....

23(c) 24 × 541 (1 mark)

……………………………………………………………………………………………

24 In the diagrams below, the square and rectangle have the same perimeter. The square has an area of 144 cm²

The length of the rectangle is three times the width of the rectangle.

Work out the length of the rectangle.

……………………………………………………………………………………………
……………………………………………………………………………………………
……………………………………………………………………………………………
……………………………………………………………………………………………
……………………………………………………………………………………………
……………………………………………………………………………………………

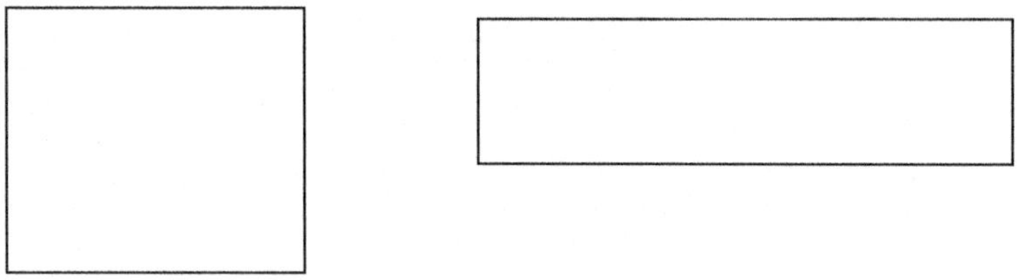

Answer………………………………. (2 marks)

25 A tennis club has 240 members.

$\frac{1}{5}$ of the members are women.

$\frac{2}{5}$ of the members are men.

The rest of the members are children.

25(a) What percentage of the members are children?

……………………………………………………………………………………………
……………………………………………………………………………………………
……………………………………………………………………………………………

Answer………………………………. (2 marks)

25(b) How many of the members are women?

....

....

....

  Answer................................ (2 marks)

25(c) How many of the members are men?

....

....

....

  Answer................................ (2 marks)

26 In the diagram below (not to scale), find the angles marked x and y.

....

....

....

....

....

....

  Answer................................ (2 marks)

27 Draw all the lines of symmetry on each of these shapes.

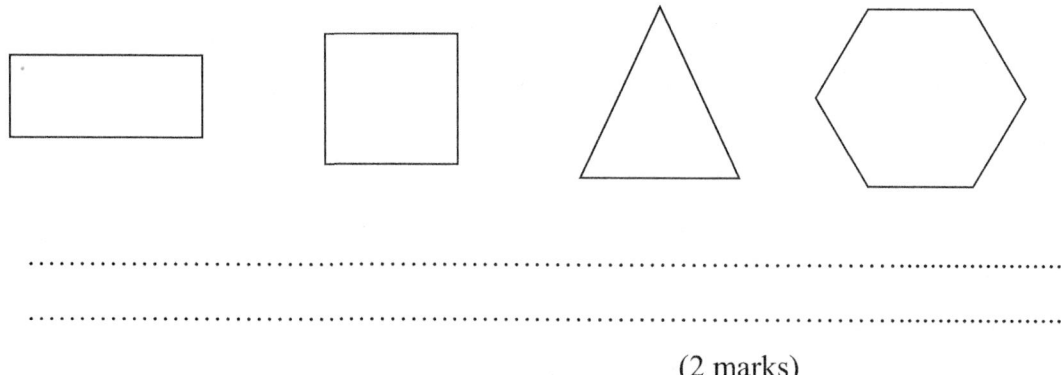

....
....

(2 marks)

28 Draw the reflection of this triangle in the mirror line shown.

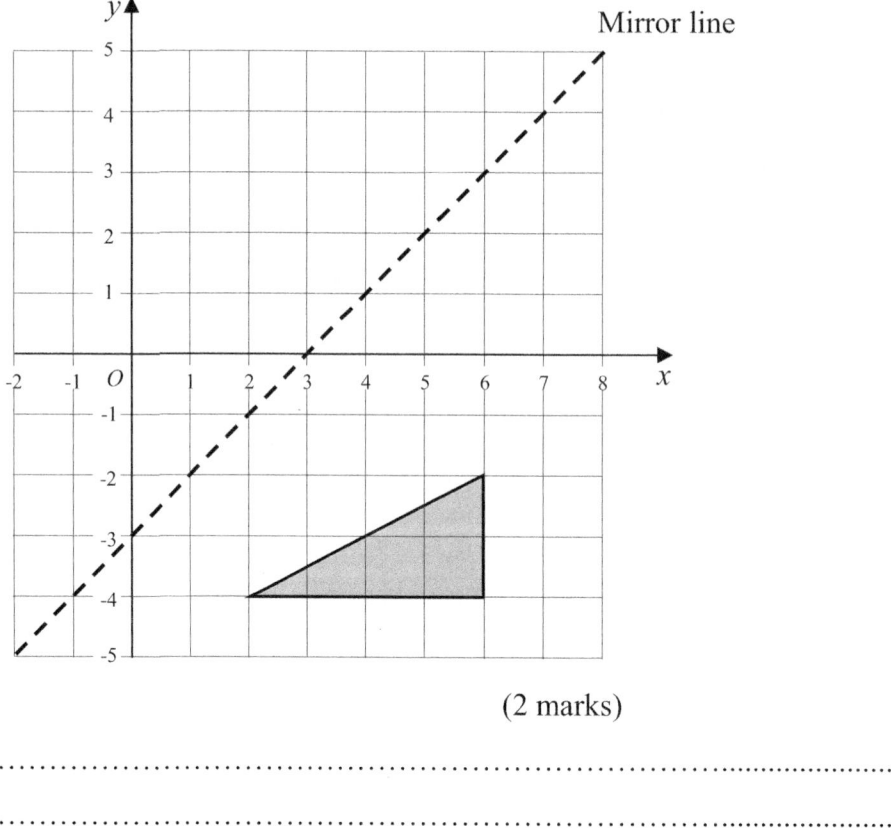

(2 marks)

....
....
....

29   The four candidates in an election were A, B, C and D.

The pie chart shows the proportion of votes for each candidate.

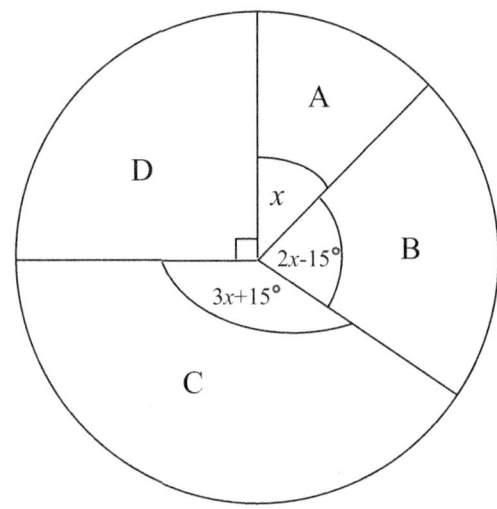

29(a)   Work out the value of x

....
....
....

Answer…………………………….   (2 marks)

29(b)   Work out the percentage of the votes for candidate A.

....
....
....

Answer…………………………….   (2 marks)

30   Can you find numbers to replace A, B and C in this sum?

(A, B and C are all different numbers)

```
      A A
      B B
  +   C C
  ─────────
      C B A
  ─────────
```

Answer…………………………….   (2 marks)

Paper 4

Materials

For this paper you must have:
- Pen, pencil, eraser and ruler.

Time allowed

1 hour.

Instructions

- Aim to complete as much as you can in the time given, without making mistakes.
- You must answer the questions in the space provided.
- Show all your working. You may be awarded marks for correct working even if your final answer is incorrect, and a correct answer unsupported by correct working may not receive full marks.
- Diagrams are not accurately drawn, unless otherwise indicated.
- Calculators are **NOT** allowed.

Information

- There are 30 questions on this paper
- The marks for questions are shown in brackets.
- The maximum mark is 100.

Advice

- Read each question carefully before you start to answer it.
- Keep an eye on the time.
- Don't worry if you don't complete the paper. If you get stuck, just go on to the next question and if you have time at the end come back to the one(s) you left.

1   Arrange the following numbers from smallest to largest.

    $\frac{1}{3}$ 0.305   0.33 $\frac{3}{10}$

    ....
    ....
    ....

            Answer................................   (2 marks)

2   Put a circle around each prime number.

    3   4   5   6   7   8

    ....
    ....

                                              (2 marks)

3(a) Work out $\frac{1}{4}$ of 96

    ....
    ....
    ....

            Answer................................   (2 marks)

3(b) Work out of $\frac{1}{2}$ of $\frac{1}{3}$ of $\frac{1}{4}$ of 96

    ....
    ....
    ....

            Answer................................   (2 marks)

4   Write the next two numbers in each sequence:

4(a) 100, 94, 88, 82, ... , ...

    ....
    ....

            Answer................................   (2 marks)

10

4(b)   1, 2, 4, 7, 11, ... , ...

....

....

   Answer............................ (2 marks)

5   Jack is now twice his sister's age. In 5 years' time Jack will be 11. How old will his sister be then?

....

....

....

   Answer............................ (3 marks)

6   The pie chart shows data collected in a survey by a PE teacher about the favourite sports of a group of school children.

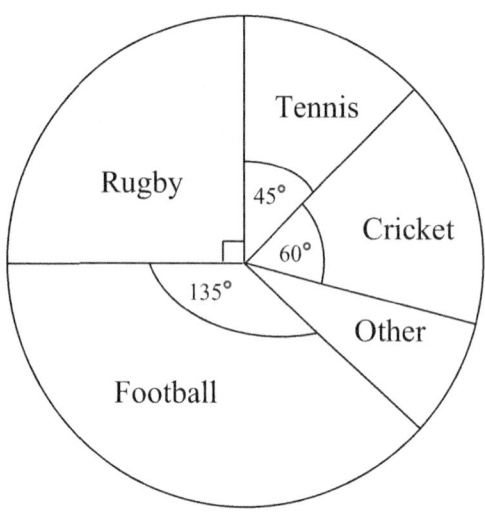

6(a)   Write down the fraction of the school children who liked cricket.
   Give your answer in the simplest form.

....

....

....

   Answer............................ (3 marks)

8

6(b) A total of 72 children were asked to complete the survey. Calculate how many children preferred tennis.

....
....
....

    Answer……………………….   (3 marks)

7 Jack and Emma are on their bicycles and start 60 miles apart on a road, riding towards each other. Jack is travelling at 20 mph, while Emma is travelling at 10 mph. They set off at the same time and keep moving at constant speeds until they meet.

7(a) Work out the distance that each rider has cycled by the time they meet.

....
....
....
....
....
....

    Answer……………………….   (2 marks)

7(b) Write down the time taken for them to meet.

....
....
....

    Answer……………………….   (2 marks)

8   How many tiles shaped like this: 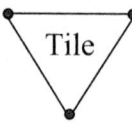 Tile

    are needed to cover the figure below?

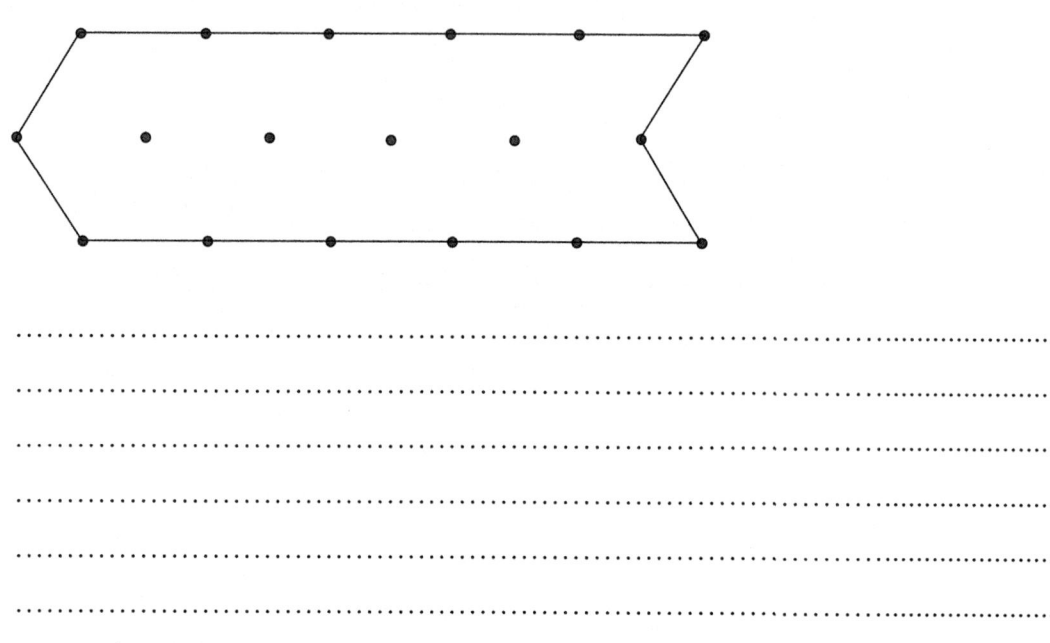

    ....
    ....
    ....
    ....
    ....
    ....

        Answer……………………….   (3 marks)

9   Label each arrow with the value indicated on the scale.

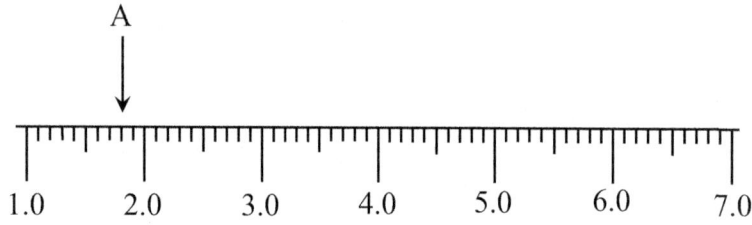

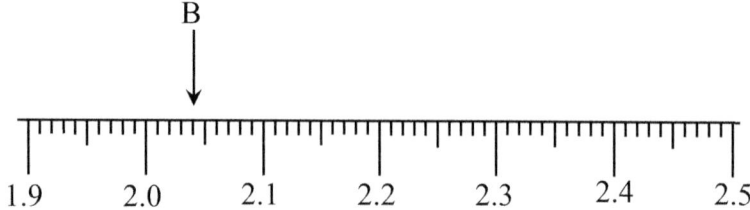

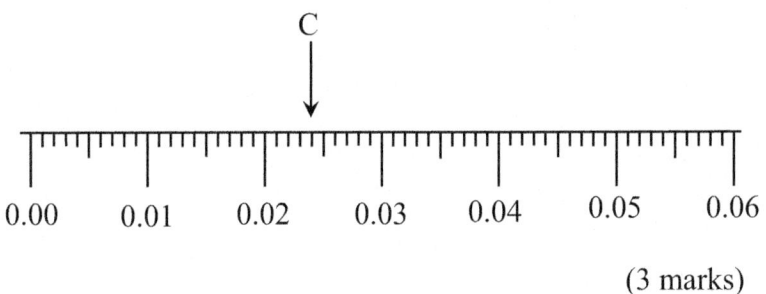

(3 marks)

10   In a class there are 30 children, the ratio of number of boys to number of girls is 3:2. Work out how many boys are in the class.

....

....

....

         Answer…………………………….   (3 marks)

11   A bottle of orange cordial makes enough drink to fill 40 glasses when it is diluted in the ratio 1 part cordial to 4 parts water. How many glasses of drink would a bottle of cordial make if it is diluted in the ratio 1 part cordial to 5 parts water?

....

....

....

         Answer…………………………….   (3 marks)

12   Which of these nets would fold to make a closed cube? Circle the appropriate letters.

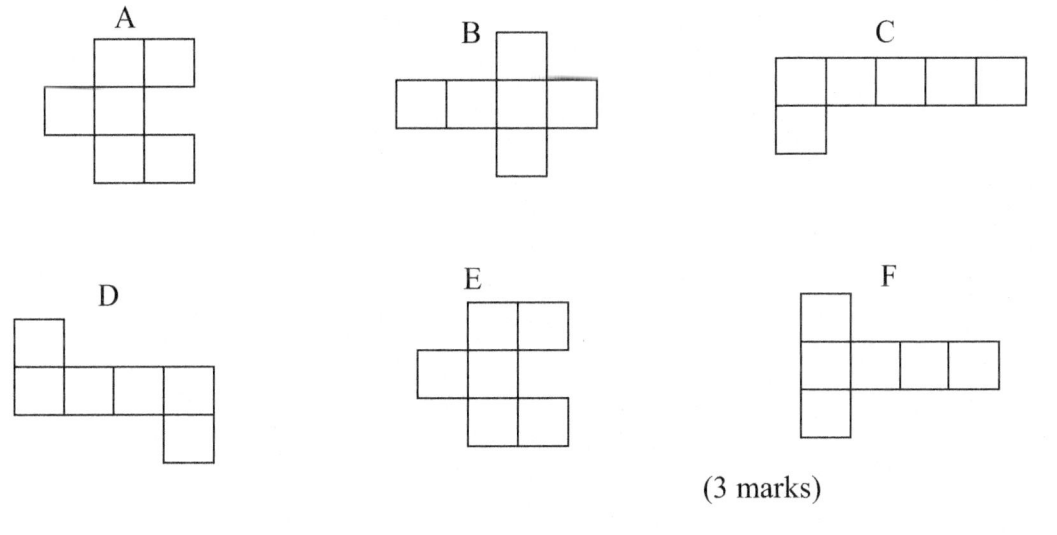

(3 marks)

13   Complete the figures below. The dotted line is the line of symmetry

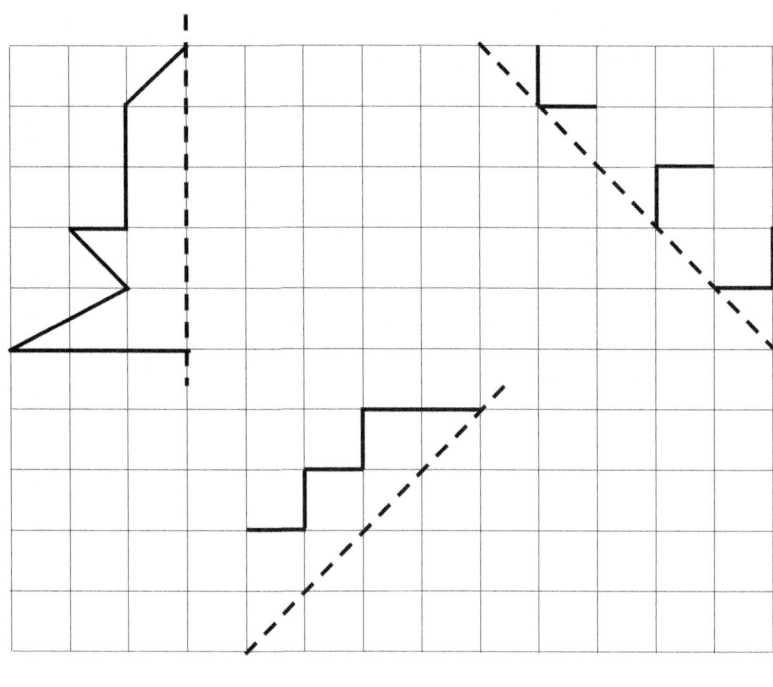

(3 marks)

14   What is the order of rotational symmetry of these shapes?

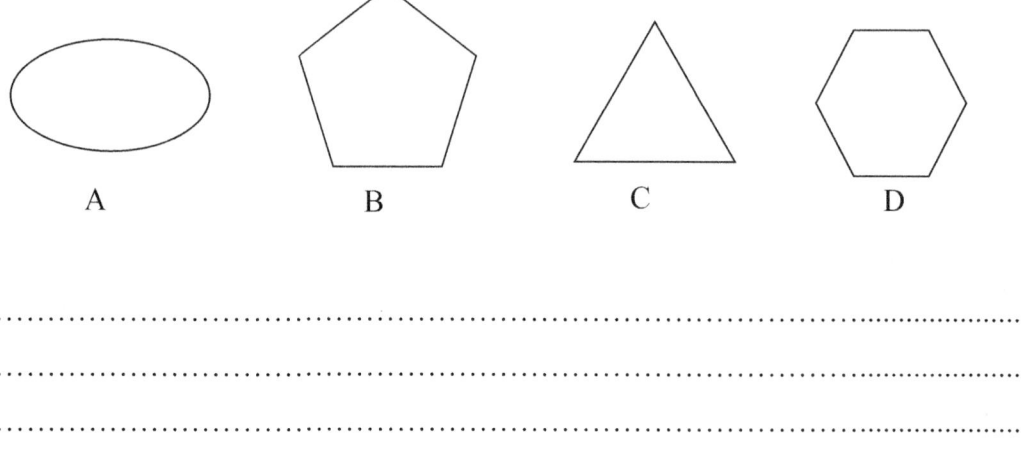

....
....
....

   Answer................................   (2 marks)

15   Jack has 75 small wooden cubes, each measuring 1cm×1cm ×1cm. He arranges them all so that they form a cuboid. Given that the perimeter of the base of the cuboid is 16 cm, what is its height?

   ....
   ....
   ....
   ....
   ....

   Answer………………………………   (3 marks)

16   In a group of 60 girls, each one is either blonde or brunette and is either blue-eyed or brown-eyed. 15 are blue-eyed blondes, 40 are brunettes, and 26 are brown-eyed. How many are brown-eyed brunettes?

   ....
   ....
   ....
   ....
   ....
   ....
   ....
   ....

   Answer………………………………   (3 marks)

17   Here are three numbers and two operations on five cards.

   | ÷ | + | 3 | 7 | 36 |

   Arrange the cards below to give the answer 19.

   | | | | | | = 19

   (2 marks)

18 A piece of cable 48 cm long is bent into the shape of a rectangle. If the length of the rectangle is 3 times its width, what is its area?

....

....

....

....

....

....

Answer................................ (3 marks)

19 The sum of the all the whole numbers from 1 to 100 inclusive is 5050. Work out the sum of the whole numbers from 2 and 101 inclusive.

....

....

....

Answer................................ (3 marks)

20 Jack thinks of a number.

He multiplies that number by 5. Then he subtracts 15. Then he divides by 3. Finally he adds 15. His answer is 35.

What number did Jack originally think of?

....

....

....

Answer................................ (3 marks)

21 Find the value of for each of the following equations

21(a) $3x - 8 = 13$

....

....

....

Answer................................ (2 marks)

11

21(b) $3(2x-5) = 21$

....
....
....

Answer.............................. (2 marks)

21(c) $\dfrac{2x}{3} + 3 = 15$

....
....
....

Answer.............................. (2 marks)

22 Each square is one square unit. What is the area of the shaded hexagon?

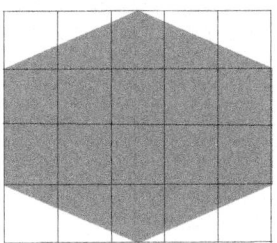

....
....
....

Answer.............................. (3 marks)

23 Emma, Jack and Mark share some money. Emma gets twice as much as Jack and three times as much as Mark. If they get £44.00 in total, how much do they each get? If Mark has 2 portions of the money, Jack would have 3 portions of the money, and Emma would have 6 portions of the money. Therefore £44.00 can be divided into 11 portions.

....

....

....

Answer................................ (3 marks)

24 A ball is dropped from a height of 12 metres. It bounces off the floor to half its original height. How far will the ball have travelled when it reaches the floor for the third time?

....

....

....

....

....

....

Answer................................ (3 marks)

25 Consecutive numbers are one apart.

25(a) Find three consecutive numbers with a sum of 48.

....

....

....

....

....

....

Answer................................ (3 marks)

25(b) Find three more consecutive numbers which give 504 when multiplied together.

....

....

....

     Answer………………………..   (3 marks)

26   The scale of a map is such that 3 cm on the map represents an actual distance of 15 km.

26(a)   Express the scale of the map as a ratio in the form 1: n where n is a whole number.

....

....

....

     Answer………………………..   (2 marks)

26(b)   The actual park is 20 km by 30 km. What are its dimensions in cm on the map?

....

....

....

     Answer………………………..   (2 marks)

27   In a sale, normal prices were reduced by 25%

27(a)   The normal price of a computer was £800

Work out the sale price of the computer.

....

....

     Answer………………………..   (2 marks)

27(b)   The normal price of a TV was reduced by £125

Work out the normal price of the TV.

....

....

     Answer………………………..   (2 marks)

28 I got 80% on a 10-problem test, 65% on a 20-problem test and 70% on a 30-problem test.

If the three tests are combined into one 60-problem test, what percentage is my overall score?

....

....

....

Answer……………………….   (3 marks)

29 Jack organised a quiz night in the toy room. He asked 25 questions.

For each correct answer you gained 4 points.

For each incorrect answer you lost 2 points.

For each question you did not attempt you scored 0 points.

Emma answered all but one of the questions and got a score of 66 points.

How many correct answers did she have?

....

....

....

....

....

Answer……………………….   (3 marks)

30 At a busy railway station trains leave from platform 6 every 6 minutes and from platform 8 every 8 minutes. Trains leave from both platforms at 15:57.

When do trains next leave both platforms at the same time?

....

....

....

....

....

Answer……………………….   (3 marks)

Paper 1 solutions

1(a) $9999 + 777 + 33 + 1$

$9999 + 777 + 33 + 1 = (9999 + 1) + (777 + 33) = 10000 + 810 = 10810$

Answer   10810   (1 mark)

Alternative method:

```
      9 9 9 9
        7 7 7
+         3 3
              1
    ─────────
    1 0 8 1 0
    ─────────
        1 2 2
```

1(b) $437 - 229$

$437 - 229 = 400 + 37 - 200 - 29 = 400 - 200 + 37 - 29 = 200 + 8 = 208$

Answer   208   (1 mark)

Alternative method:

$$\begin{array}{r} 4\overset{2}{\cancel{3}}\overset{1}{7} \\ -\ 2\ 2\ 9 \\ \hline 2\ 0\ 8 \\ \hline \end{array}$$

$99 \times 38 = 100 \times 38 - 38 = 3800 - 38 = 3762$

2(a) 99×38

$99 \times 38 = 100 \times 38 - 38 = 3800 - 38 = 3762$

Answer   3762   (1 mark)

Alternative method:

$$\begin{array}{r} \overset{7}{}9\ 9 \\ \times\ \ \ 3\ 8 \\ \hline 7\ 9\ 2 \\ 2\ 9\ 7\ \\ \hline 3\ 7\ 6\ 2 \\ \hline \end{array}$$

3

2(b) $71.1 \div 9$

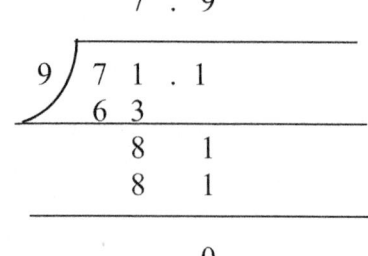

　　　　　Answer　　　7.9　　　　　(1 mark)

Alternative method: $71.1 \div 9 = (71.1 \div 3) \div 3 = 23.7 \div 3 = 7.9$

3(a) $\dfrac{5}{8} + \dfrac{3}{16}$

$\dfrac{5}{8} + \dfrac{3}{16} = \dfrac{10}{16} + \dfrac{3}{16} = \dfrac{13}{16}$

　　　　　Answer　　　$\dfrac{13}{16}$　　　　　(1 mark)

3(b) $1\dfrac{1}{4} - \dfrac{3}{8}$

$1\dfrac{1}{4} - \dfrac{3}{8} = 1\dfrac{2}{8} - \dfrac{3}{8} = \dfrac{10}{8} - \dfrac{3}{8} = \dfrac{7}{8}$

　　　　　Answer　　　$\dfrac{7}{8}$　　　　　(2 marks)

4(a) What number must be added to 59 to give the result 3100?

$3100 - 59 = 3000 + 100 - 59 = 3000 + 41 = 3041$

　　　　　Answer　　　3041　　　　　(2 marks)

4(b) Write down any fraction between $\dfrac{1}{3}$ and $\dfrac{1}{2}$.

As $\dfrac{1}{3} \approx 0.333$, $\dfrac{1}{2} = 0.5$, 0.4 is between them.

$0.4 = \dfrac{4}{10} = \dfrac{2}{5}$

　　　　　Answer　　　$\dfrac{2}{5}$　　　　　(2 marks)

8

Alternative method:

$\dfrac{\dfrac{1}{3}+\dfrac{1}{2}}{2} = \dfrac{\dfrac{2}{6}+\dfrac{3}{6}}{2} = \dfrac{\dfrac{5}{6}}{2} = \dfrac{5}{12}$, this value, $\dfrac{5}{12}$, is also between $\dfrac{1}{3}$ and $\dfrac{1}{2}$

5(a) Work out $(58+57+56+55)-(57+56+55+54)$

$(58+\cancel{57}+\cancel{56}+\cancel{55})-(\cancel{57}+\cancel{56}+\cancel{55}+54) = 58 - 54 = 4$

Answer   4   (2 marks)

5(b) What is the greatest whole number that you can make using the digits 5, 4, 9 and 8? Use each digit only once.

Answer   9854   (2 marks)

6(a) What is 25% of 40?

$25\% \times 40 = \dfrac{25}{100} \times 40 = \dfrac{1}{4} \times 40 = 10$

Answer   10   (2 marks)

6(b) What is 40% of 25?

$40\% \times 25 = \dfrac{40}{100} \times 25 = \dfrac{10}{25} \times 25 = 10$

Answer   10   (2 marks)

6(c) What is 50% of 25% of 40?

$50\% \times 25\% \times 40 = \dfrac{1}{2} \times \dfrac{1}{4} \times 40 = 5$

Answer   5   (2 marks)

7   Arrange the digits 7, 6, 5, and 4 so that the resulting number is closest to five thousand.

There are two numbers which are close to five thousand, 4765 and 5467.

$5000 - 4765 = 235$, $5467 - 5000 = 467$

∴ 4765 is closest to five thousand.

   Answer   4765   (2 marks)

8   Write the correct number in each box.

$$\frac{3}{5} = \frac{\Box}{15} = \frac{12}{\Box} = \frac{\Box}{25} = \frac{27}{\Box}$$ (2 marks)

$$\frac{3}{5} = \frac{9}{15} = \frac{12}{20} = \frac{15}{25} = \frac{27}{45}$$

9   Circle the two numbers from the list below which have a total of 0.15

   0.1   0.09   0.5   0.14   0.06   (2 marks)

   0.1   (0.09)   0.5   0.14   (0.06)

$0.09 + 0.06 = 0.15$

10   Write the correct number in each box.

10(a) $200 = 40 \div \Box$ (2 marks)

$200 = 40 \div 0.2$

10(b) $\dfrac{63.2}{\Box} = 632$ (2 marks)

$\dfrac{63.2}{0.1} = 632$

10(c) $73.5 \times \Box = 7.35$ (2 marks)

$73.5 \times 0.1 = 7.35$

12

10(d) $100 = 35 \div \boxed{}$ (2 marks)

$100 = 35 \div \boxed{0.35}$

11 Emma has four number cards:

$\boxed{1}$ $\boxed{2}$ $\boxed{8}$ $\boxed{9}$

She arranges them to form two 2 digit numbers. She multiplies the numbers together.

Which two 2 digit numbers give the largest answer?

Either 81×92 or 82×91 gives largest possible answer.

$81 \times 92 - 82 \times 91 = 81 \times 91 + 81 - (81 \times 91 + 91) = 81 - 91 = -10 < 0$

$\therefore 82 \times 91$ gives the largest answer.

Answer   82 and 91   (2 marks)

12(a) $2 - 1\frac{7}{11}$

$2 - 1\frac{7}{11} = 1\frac{11}{11} - 1\frac{7}{11} = \frac{4}{11}$

Answer $\frac{4}{11}$ (2 marks)

12(b) $\frac{1}{5} + \frac{2}{15}$

$\frac{1}{5} + \frac{2}{15} = \frac{3}{15} + \frac{2}{15} = \frac{5}{15} = \frac{1}{3}$

Answer $\frac{1}{3}$ (2 marks)

13 Shortcrust pastry is made using flour and fat in the ratio 2:1.

How many grams of flour are needed to make 450 grams of shortcrust pastry?

The proportion of flour is $\frac{2}{3}$.

$450 \times \frac{2}{3} = 300$

Answer   300 grams   (2 marks)

$\boxed{10}$

14(a) Find the area of the rectangle shown below.

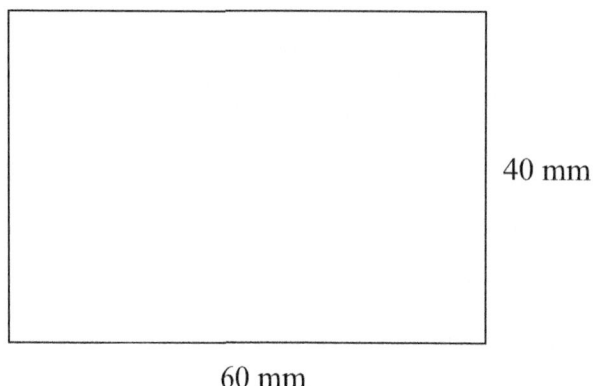

$40 \times 60 = 2400$

Answer   2400 mm²   (2 marks)

14(b) Jack cuts the rectangle up into an exact number of right-angled triangles, each with sides as shown in the diagram below.

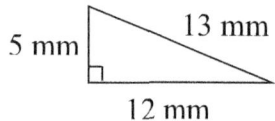

Calculate the number of triangles that he can cut from the rectangle.

$\dfrac{40}{5} = 8$, $\dfrac{60}{12} = 5$

∴ The number of triangles that he can cut from the rectangle can be calculated as follows:

$8 \times 5 \times 2 = 80$

Answer   80   (2 marks)

14(c) What fraction of the figure is shaded?

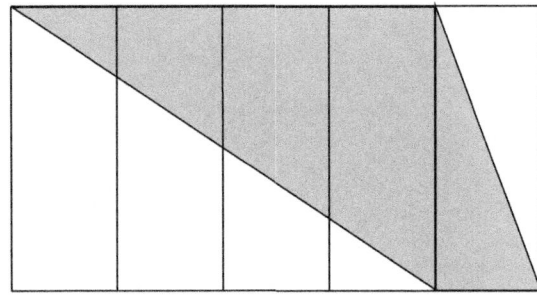

Answer $\frac{1}{2}$ (2 marks)

15   Find the size of angle 'a' in the diagram below.

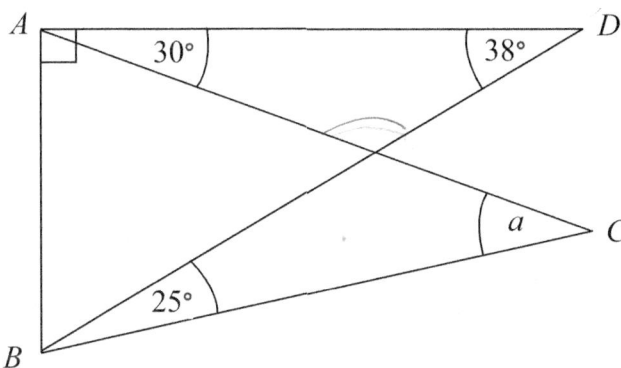

As $\angle DAB = 90°$, $\angle CAB = 90° - 30° = 60°$

In the right-angled triangle DAB, $\angle DBA = 90° - 38° = 52°$

In the triangle ABC, $a = 180° - \angle CAB - \angle DBA - \angle DBC = 180° - 60° - 52° - 25° = 43°$

Answer   43°   (2 marks)

16(a) Emma takes 38 minutes to travel to work each morning. She leaves home at 8.15 a.m. What time does she arrive at work?

$8\,h\,15\,min + 38\,min = 8\,h\,53\,min$

Answer   8.53 a.m.   (2 marks)

16(b) The journey home in the evening takes the same time. She arrives home at 6.24 p.m. At what time did she leave work?

$6\,h\,24\,min - 38\,min = 5\,h\,84\,min - 38\,min = 5\,h\,46\,min$

Answer   5.46 p.m.   (2 marks)

17 My age is a multiple of 9. Next year it will be a multiple of 5. I am more than 30 years old, but less than 80. How old am I?

My age is a multiple of 9, it could be 36, 45, 54, 63 or 72.

Next year it will be a multiple of 5, only "54+1" is a multiple of 5 for the above numbers.

∴ I am 54 years old.

Answer   54 years old   (2 marks)

18 $805 = a \times b \times c$, where a, b and c are prime numbers, with c is bigger than b, and b bigger than a.

Find a, b and c

It is easy to find that 805 can be divided by 5.

$805 \div 5 = 161$.

In the same way, you can find that 161 can be divided by 7.

$161 \div 7 = 23$

∴ $a = 5$, $b = 7$, $c = 23$

Answer $a = 5$, $b = 7$, $c = 23$ (3 marks)

19 The figure below is made up of ten equal squares. The perimeter of the figure is 112 cm.

What is the area of one of the squares?

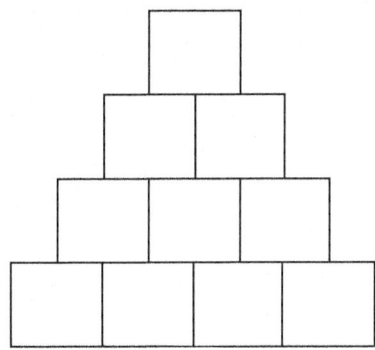

If the length of a side of the square is x, $112 \text{ cm} = 16x \Rightarrow x = 7 \text{ cm}$

The area of one of the squares can be calculated as follows:

$(7 \text{ cm})^2 = 49 \text{ cm}^2$

Answer   49 cm²   (3 marks)

20 A bus has 35 passengers on board. At the first stop two fifths get off and then 7 people get on. At the next stop a quarter of the people remaining on the bus get off and then 13 get on.

How many passengers are there on the bus now?

At the first stop, the number of passengers is: $35 - \frac{2}{5} \times 35 + 7 = 28$

At the next stop, the number of passengers is: $28 - \frac{1}{4} \times 28 + 13 = 34$

Answer   34   (3 marks)

21(a) Find two numbers which when multiplied together make a hundred. Neither of the two numbers must use any 0s.

$4 \times 25 = 100$

Answer   4 and 25   (2 marks)

21(b) Find two numbers which when multiplied together make a thousand. Once again, neither of the two numbers must use any 0s.

$1000 = 25 \times 40 = 25 \times 5 \times 8 = 125 \times 8$

Answer   8 and 125   (2 marks)

10

22(a) I turn 50 degrees clockwise, 80 degrees anticlockwise and finally 90 degrees clockwise. If I want to return to my original position by turning through the smallest possible angle, in which direction should I turn and what should the angle be?

If anticlockwise turn is positive, the clockwise turn is negative.

Therefore the angle, which I have turned, can be calculated as follows:

$-50° + 80° - 90° = -60°$

If I want to return to my original position, I need to turn $60°$ anticlockwise.

    Answer   60 degrees anticlockwise   (2 marks)

22(b) If I face West and turn 270 degrees clockwise, in which direction am I now facing?

Sketch the diagram which I face West and turn 270 degrees clockwise as follows.

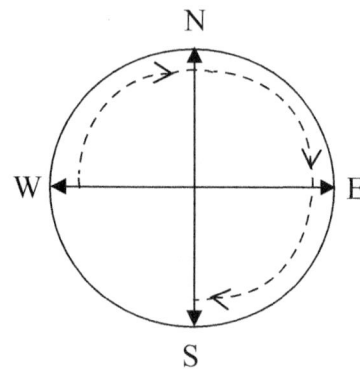

From the diagram, it is easy to see that I am facing South now, after I turn 270 degrees clockwise.

    Answer   South   (2 marks)

23 In the boxes, write the numbers that their arrows are pointing to.

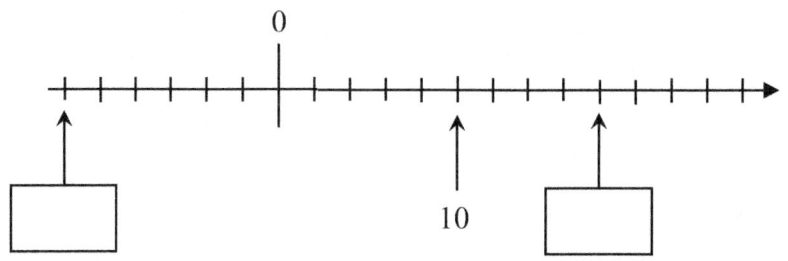

Negative numbers always lie on the left side of zero

Positive numbers always lie on the right side of zero

The space between the two lines is 2 units.

Therefore the boxes can be filled by numbers as follows.

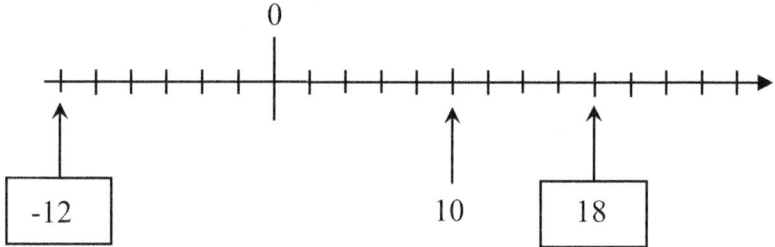

(2 marks)

24 Look at the number pattern below:

$1^2 + 3 = 4$

$2^2 + 5 = 9$

$3^2 + 7 = 16$

24(a) Fill in the next two lines of the pattern,

____ + ____ = ____

____ + ____ = ____

(2 marks)

$4^2 + 9 = 25$

$5^2 + 11 = 36$

4

24(b) Complete the following line which comes later in the pattern.

____ + ____ = 144

$144 = 12^2$

$\therefore 11^2 + 23 = 144$

(2 marks)

25 ABCD is a rectangle. What is the area of the shaded region?

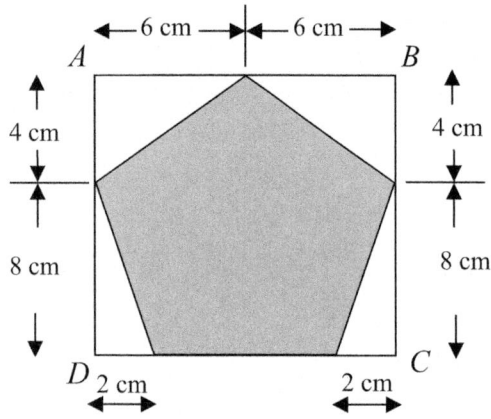

The area of the shaded region can be calculated as follows:

$12 \times 12 - 2 \times \dfrac{4 \times 6}{2} - 2 \times \dfrac{2 \times 8}{2} = 144 - 24 - 16 = 104$

Answer   104 cm²   (3 marks)

26 There are 27 cubes, and each has a surface area of 8 cm²

They are joined together to make a big cube.

What could the surface area of the big cube be?

The cube has 6 faces, and each face of the big cube contains 9 faces of the small cubes.

Therefore the surface area of the big cube can be calculated as follows:

$6 \times 9 \times \dfrac{8}{6} = 72$

Answer   72 cm²   (3 marks)

27(a) Given that Jack eats $\frac{3}{5}$ of a cake and his friend, Jerry, eats $\frac{1}{4}$ of the cake, what fraction of the cake is left?

$1 - \frac{3}{5} - \frac{1}{4} = 1 - (\frac{12}{20} + \frac{5}{20}) = 1 - \frac{17}{20} = \frac{3}{20}$

Answer $\frac{3}{20}$ (2 marks)

27(b) Given that Jack's piece of cake weighed 150 grams, what was the weight of the whole cake?

$150 \div \frac{3}{5} = 150 \times \frac{5}{3} = 250$

Answer   250 grams   (2 marks)

27(c) Jack uses 650 g of sugar from a 3.5 kg packet. How many kilograms of sugar are left?

$3.5 - 0.65 = 2.85$

Answer   2.85 kg   (2 marks)

28   25 students have taken an exam and the mean number of marks is recorded as 82. The examiner subsequently awards 5 additional marks to 9 of the students and takes away 3 marks from 10 other students.

What will the new mean mark be?

The new mean mark is calculated as follows:

$82 + \frac{5 \times 9 - 3 \times 10}{25} = 82.6$

Answer   82.6   (2 marks)

29   I am thinking of a number less than 60.

When my number is divided by 4, it gives remainder 2.

When my number is divided by 5, it gives remainder 3.

When my number is divided by 6, it gives remainder 4.

What number am I thinking of?

When my number is divided by 4, it gives remainder 2.

It could be 6, 10, 14, 18, 22, 26, 30, 34, 38, 42, 46, 50, 54, 58.

When my number is divided by 5, it gives remainder 3.

It could be 8, 13, 18, 23, 28, 33, 38, 43, 48, 53, 58.

When my number is divided by 6, it gives remainder 4.

It could be 10, 16, 22, 28, 34, 40, 46, 52, 58.

Therefore the number, which I am thinking of, is 58.

Answer   58   (3 marks)

30   A car leaves Birmingham New Street travelling 50 miles per hour. An hour later, a second car leaves Birmingham New Street following the first car, travelling 70 miles per hour.

How long will it take the second car to overtake the first car, after leaving Birmingham New Street?

The second car takes x hours to overtake the first car, after leaving Birmingham New Street.

$x \times 70 = (x+1) \times 50 \Rightarrow 70x - 50x = 50 \Rightarrow x = 2.5$

Answer   2.5 hours   (3 marks)

Paper 2 solutions

1(a) What number is 1000 more than 45678?

$1000 + 45678 = 46678$

    Answer   46678   (1 mark)

1(b) What number is 0·02 more than 14·99?

$0.02 + 14.99 = 15.01$

    Answer   15.01   (1 mark)

2(a)

```
    8 8 8 8            8 8 8 8
      7 7 7              7 7 7
+       3 3        +       3 3
          2                  2
  ─────────          ─────────
                     9 7 0 0
  ─────────          ─────────
                       1 2 2
```

    Answer   9700   (2 marks)

2(b)

```
    5 4 3 2 1            ³5 ²4̸ ¹3̸ ²̸ 1
  - 1 2 3 4 5          - 1 2 3 4 5
  ───────────          ─────────────
                         4 1 9 7 6
  ───────────          ─────────────
```

    Answer   41976   (2 marks)

3(a) 596×35

```
        ⁴ ³
      5 9 6
  ×     3 5
  ─────────
      2 9 8 0
      1 7 8 8
  ─────────
      2 0 8 6 0
```

    Answer   20860   (2 marks)

Alternative method:

$596 \times 35 = 600 \times 35 - 4 \times 35 = 21000 - 140 = 20860$

8

3(b)   2024 ÷ 8

```
        2 5 3
      ┌───────
    8 │ 2 0 2 4
        1 6
        ───
          4 2
          4 0
          ───
            2 4
            2 4
            ───
              0
```

Answer   253   (2 marks)

Alternative method:

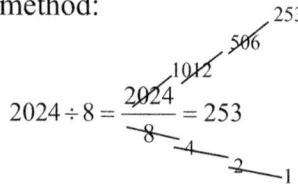

$$2024 \div 8 = \frac{2024}{8} = 253$$

Note: Numerator and denominator are divided by 2 until that the denominator is 1.

4   What is half of $45\frac{1}{2}$?

$$\frac{1}{2} \times 45\frac{1}{2} = \frac{1}{2} \times 44\frac{3}{2} = 22\frac{3}{4}$$

Answer $22\frac{3}{4}$ (2 marks)

5(a)   4444 p   =   £..............................
        Answer   £44.44   (2 marks)

5(b)   40 cm   = ...m
        Answer   0.4 m   (2 marks)

5(c)   1 m 5 cm = ...m
        Answer   1.05 m   (2 marks)

5(d)   3 m 50 cm = ...cm
        Answer   3.5 m   (2 marks)

5(e) $3\frac{1}{3}$ hr = ...minutes

Answer   200 minutes   (2 marks)

6   Arrange the following decimals from the smallest to the largest

1.4   1.42   1.04   1.402

Answer   1.04 1.4 1.402 1.42   (2 marks)

7   Jack is three times as heavy as Emma. If Jack is 8 kg heavier than Emma.
What is the weight of Jack in kg?

The weight of Emma is E kg

The weight of Jack is (E+8) kg

Jack is three times as heavy as Emma: 2E = 8 $\Rightarrow$ E = 4

The weight of Jack = (E+8) kg = 12 kg,

(or the weight of Jack = (3×E) kg = 12 kg)

Answer   12 kg   (2 marks)

8   A carpet which measures 6 m × 4 m covers 60% of the floor area of a rectangular room. The length of the room is 8 m. What is its width?

The floor area of a rectangular room is $\frac{6\,m \times 4\,m}{60\%} = 40\,m^2$

Its width is $\frac{40\,m^2}{8\,m} = 5\,m$

Answer   5 m   (2 marks)

9   A mosaic pattern is arranged as shown using balls.

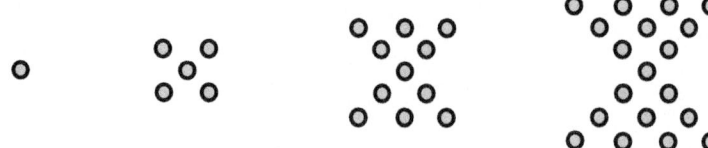

Any number in this sequence can be found as follows:

1st Pattern $(1 \times 2) - 1 = 1$

2nd Pattern $(2 \times 3) - 1 = 5$

3rd Pattern $(3 \times 4) - 1 = 11$

9(a)   Fill in the next two lines of the pattern,

____ - ____ = ____   (1 mark)

$(4 \times 5) - 1 = 19$

____ - ____ = ____   (1 mark)

$(5 \times 6) - 1 = 29$

9(b)   Complete the following line which comes later in the pattern.

____ - ____ = 109   (2 marks)

$(10 \times 11) - 1 = 109$

10   Write the following events in order, with the most probable (i.e. most likely) first and the least probable (i.e. least likely) last. Give your answer as a sequence of letters, e.g. BACED.

A: Being born on the weekend;

B: Being born on Christmas Eve;

C: Rolling a 4 with a fair cube die;

D: Obtaining a head when a fair coin is tossed;

E: Obtaining an even number when two odd numbers are multiplied together.

A: The probability is $\frac{2}{7}$;

B: The probability is $\frac{1}{365}$;

C: The probability is $\frac{1}{6}$;

D: The probability is $\frac{1}{2}$;

E: The probability is 0,

When two odd numbers are multiplied together, it always gives odd number.

     Answer   DACBE   (3 marks)

11 Complete the train time table below.

Route	Departs	Arrives	Journey Time
London – Birmingham	09:45		1 hr 20 min
London – Manchester	11:05	13:03	
London – Carlisle		16:12	3 hr 17 min

(3 marks)

The calculations are as follows:

$9\,h\,45\,min + 1\,h\,20\,min = 10\,h\,65\,min = 11\,h\,5\,min$, $11:05$ (Arrives)

$13\,h\,3\,min - 11\,h\,5\,min = 12\,h\,63\,min - 11\,h\,5\,min = 1\,h\,58\,min$, $1\,hr\,58\,min$ (Journey Time)

$16\,h\,12\,min - 3\,h\,17\,min = 15\,h\,72\,min - 3\,h\,17\,min = 12\,h\,55\,min$, $12:55$ (Departs)

The completed table is as follows.

Route	Departs	Arrives	Journey Time
London – Birmingham	09:45	11:05	1 hr 20 min
London – Manchester	11:05	13:03	1 hr 58 min
London – Carlisle	12:55	16:12	3 hr 17 min

12 A wire costs £1.02 per metre.

12(a) How much will it cost to buy 10 metres?

$£1.02 \times 10 = £10.20$

Answer   £10.20   (2 marks)

12(b) Jack buys a length of wire costing £25.50. How many metres does he buy?

$\dfrac{£25.50}{£1.02/m} = 25\,m$

Answer   25 m   (2 marks)

13 Five miles is the same distance as eight kilometres. Use this fact to convert 120 kilometres into miles.

$\dfrac{120}{8} \times 5 = 75$

Answer   75 miles   (2 marks)

14   There are 68 apples in a box. 25% of them are red and the rest are green. How many green apples are there in the box?

$68 \times (1 - 25\%) = 68 \times 0.75 = \dfrac{68}{4} \times 3 = 17 \times 3 = 51$

Answer   51   (2 marks)

15   Here are three lamps.

Lamp A flashes every 4 minutes. Lamp B flashes every 6 minutes. Lamp C flashes every 8 minutes. The three lamps start flashing at 10.00 a. m., at what time will they next flash together?

$4 = 2 \times 2$, $6 = 2 \times 3$, $8 = 2 \times 2 \times 2$

The lowest common multiple (LCM) of 4, 6 and 8 is:

LCM $= 2 \times 2 \times 2 \times 3 = 24$

Therefore they will next flash together in 24 minutes, which is at 10.24 a. m.

Answer   10.24 a. m.   (2 marks)

16   Cans are often stacked like this in a supermarket display.

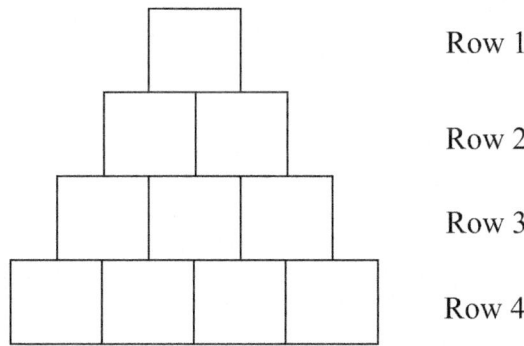

Row 1

Row 2

Row 3

Row 4

16(a)   Find the total number of cans in the first four rows.

1 + 2 + 3 + 4 = 10

Answer   10   (2 marks)

16(b)   How many rows would be needed to display 36 cans?

$36 - 10 = 26 = 5 + 6 + 7 + 8$, (4 rows can display 10 cans from part (a) above.)

Therefore 4 rows more are needed, compared to part (a). The total number of rows is 8.

Answer   8   (2 marks)

17   A cube with sides 4 cm is made from smaller cubes of side 1cm as shown.

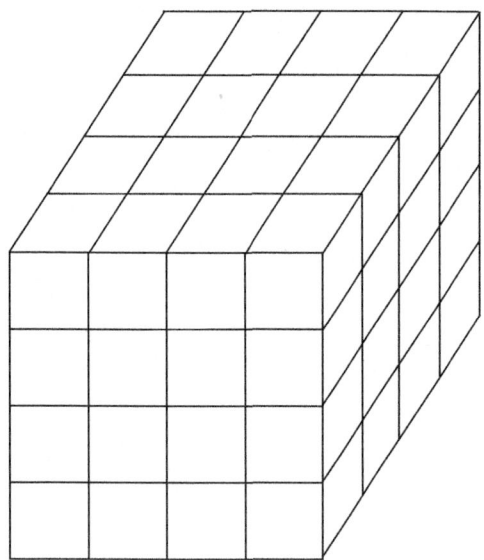

17(a)   How many small cubes are used in making the bigger cube?

$4 \times 4 \times 4 = 64$

Answer   64   (2 marks)

17(b)   If the bigger cube is painted red all over, how many small cubes will have one red face?

The bigger cube has 6 faces; each has 4 small cubes with one red face.

$6 \times 4 = 24$

Answer   24   (2 marks)

17(c)   How many small cubes will have 2 red faces?

The bigger cube has 12 edges; each edge has 2 small cubes with 2 red faces.

$12 \times 2 = 24$

Answer   24   (2 marks)

18   A large rectangle is made by joining five identical small rectangles as shown.

Diagram **NOT** accurately drawn

The perimeter of one small rectangle is 50 cm.

Work out the perimeter of the large rectangle.

The length of the small rectangle is 4 times its width.

width + length = 25 cm.

width is $\frac{1}{5} \times 25 \,\text{cm} = 5 \,\text{cm}$

length is $\frac{4}{5} \times 25 \,\text{cm} = 20 \,\text{cm}$

The perimeter of the large rectangle is $4 \times 20 + 2 \times 5 = 90$

Answer   90 cm   (2 marks)

19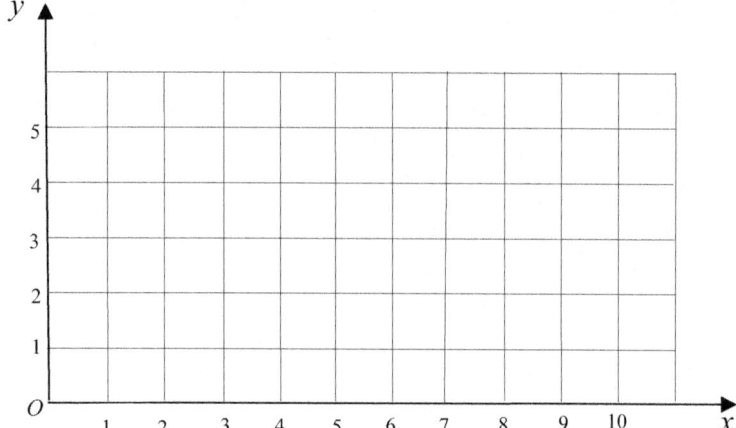

19(a) On the grid above, plot and label the points $A\,(2, 3)$, $B(4, 5)$, $C\,(8, 3)$ and $D\,(4,1)$.

(2 marks)

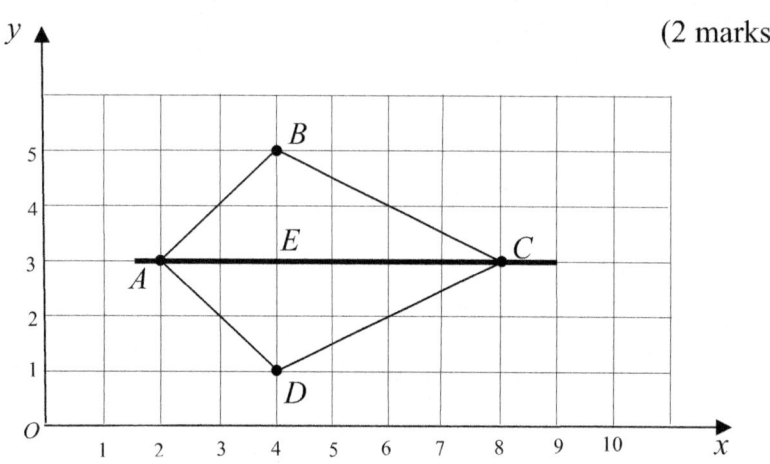

As shown on the graph.

19(b) Join *ABCD*.

(1 mark)

As shown on the graph.

19(c) What name is given to this shape?

Answer   Kite   (2 marks)

5

19(d) Find the coordinates of the point of intersection of the diagonals.

The point of intersection of the diagonals is E.

$E_x = B_x = 4$, $E_y = A_y = 3$.

It is also easy to see the coordinates of the point of intersection of the diagonals.

The coordinates of this point are (4,3), from the graph.

  Answer (4,3)   (2 marks)

19(e) Draw on any lines of symmetry.

As shown on the graph. (1 mark)

19(f) Calculate the area of $ABCD$.

$$\frac{AC \times BD}{2} = \frac{(8-2) \times (5-1)}{2} = 12$$

  Answer 12 square units (2 marks)

20 This factory was built in the year in which Jack was born. Jack was 30 years old in the 1995. How old was this factory in 2018?

$2018 - 1995 = 23$, from 1995 to 2018, 23 years passed.

In 2018, Jack's age $= 23 + 30 = 53$. The factory has the same age as Jack.

  Answer 53 years old (2 marks)

21 Along any line drawn, the numbers in the two circles at the end of a line should multiply to make the number in the square between the two circles.

Fill the remaining squares and circles with numbers obeying this rule.

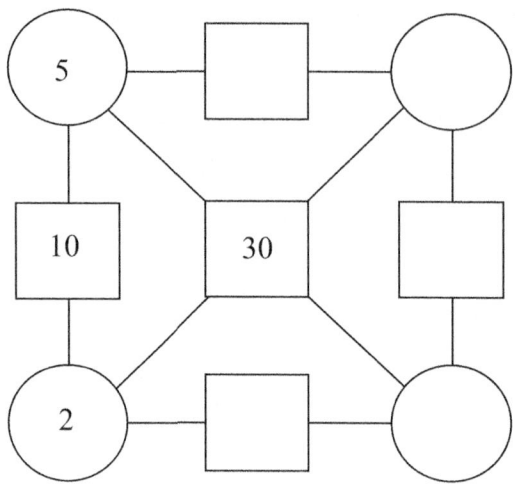

(2 marks)

The numbers are filled as shown on the diagram.

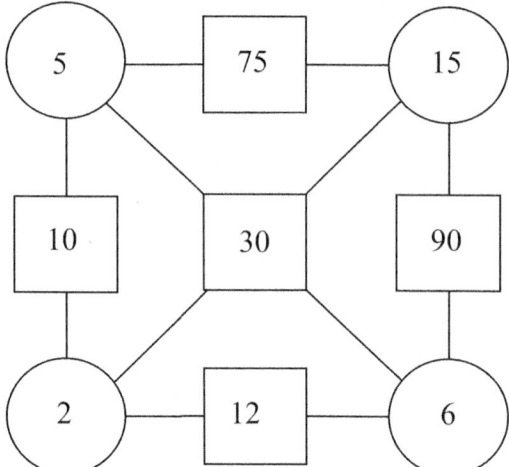

22 In a children's game you call out all the numbers from 1 to 100. You clap every time you say either a multiple of 7 or a number ending in 7. How many times would you clap?

From 1 to 100, a multiple of 7 are 7 (=1×7), 14 (=2×7), 21 (=3×7), 28 (=4×7), 35 (=5×7), 42 (=6×7), 49 (=7×7), 56 (=8×7), 63 (=9×7), 70 (=10×7), 77 (=11×7), 84 (=12×7), 91 (=13×7), 98 (=14×7). Altogether there are 14 numbers which are multiple of 7.

Numbers ending in 7 are 7, 17, 27, 37, 47, 57, 67, 77, 87, 97. Altogether there are 10 numbers which ends in 7.

7 and 77 are multiple of 7 and also end in 7.

$14 + 10 - 2 = 22$

Answer   22   (2 marks)

23 In a box of pens, one third are black, one fifth are red and the rest are blue. What fraction of the pens is blue?

$$1 - \frac{1}{3} - \frac{1}{5} = 1 - (\frac{5}{15} + \frac{3}{15}) = 1 - \frac{8}{15} = \frac{7}{15}$$

Answer $\frac{7}{15}$ (2 marks)

24 To cook a joint of beef, you leave it in the oven for 30 minutes for every kilogram it weighs, plus 20 minutes extra. Find how long you would cook a joint weighing:

24(a) 2kg

30 min× 2 + 20 min = 80 min = 1 hr 20 min

Answer   1 hr 20 min   (2 marks)

24(b) 3.5 kg

30 min× 3.5 + 20 min = 125 min = 2 hr 5 min

Answer   2 hr 5 min   (2 marks)

8

25 Six football teams play each other once. How many matches will need to be played? The following diagram shows that Team 1 has 5 matches, with Teams 2, 3, 4, 5 and 6 respectively.

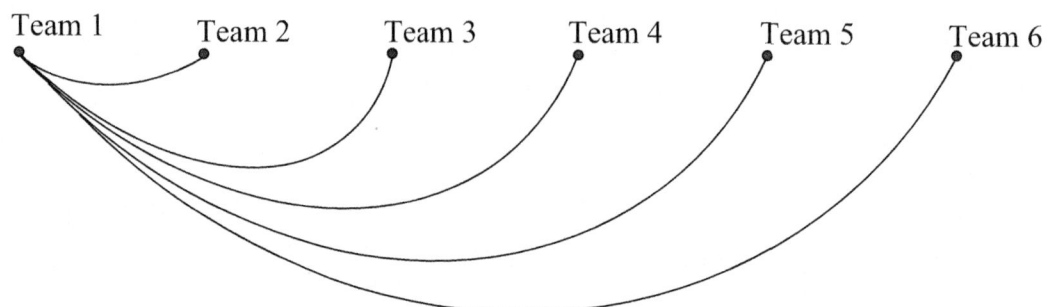

Team 2 has 4 matches, with Teams 3, 4, 5 and 6 respectively, after the matching with Team 1, by using the similar diagram, as follows:

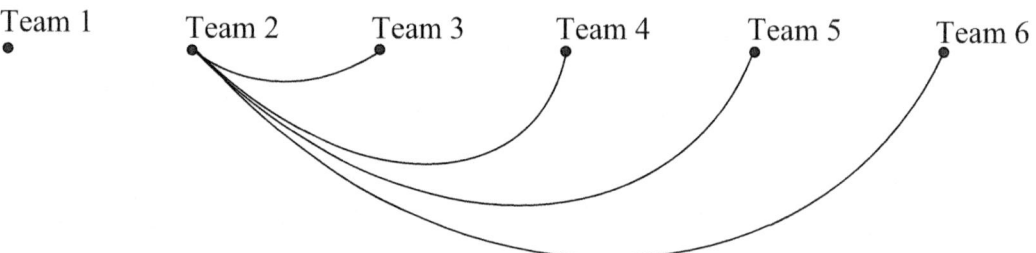

In the similar way, Team 3 has 3 matches, with Teams 4, 5 and 6, respectively, after the matching with Teams 1 and 2;

Team 4 has 2 matches, with Teams 5 and 6, respectively, after the matching with Teams 1 and 2 and 3.

Team 5 has 1 match with Team 6, after the matching with Teams 1 and 2 and 3 and 4.

Therefore the total number of the matches:

$5+4+3+2+1=15$.

Answer   15   (3 marks)

Alternative method, by using a hexagon, as follows:

Each line between the two teams represents one match each other. The number of lines is equivalent to the number of matches. Therefore counting the number of the lines would give the number of matches, 15.

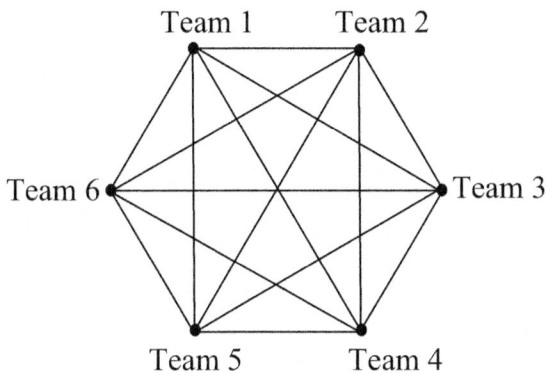

26 Write down (in simplest form) the fraction that the arrow is pointing to.

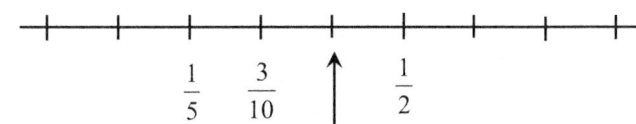

$\frac{1}{5} = 0.2$, $\frac{3}{10} = 0.3$, $\frac{1}{2} = 0.5$.

"↑" is pointing 0.4. $0.4 = \frac{4}{10} = \frac{2}{5}$

Answer $\frac{2}{5}$ (2 marks)

27 When two numbers are added together, the result is 32. When the smaller number is subtracted from the larger one, the result is 6. Find these two numbers.

The smaller number is x, the larger one is $x+6$

$x + x + 6 = 32 \Rightarrow x = 13$, the larger one is $13 + 6 = 19$

Answer   13, 19   (2 marks)

28(a) Yesterday's tomorrow is Friday.

What day is the day after tomorrow's yesterday?

Yesterday's tomorrow is Friday ⇒ Today is Friday.

The day after tomorrow's yesterday ⇒ The day after tomorrow's yesterday is Saturday.

     Answer   Saturday   (2 marks)

28(b) If March 23rd is a Monday, on what day of the week is April 2nd?

In March, there are 31 days. April 2nd is 10 days later after March 23rd. April 2nd is Thursday.

     Answer   Thursday   (2 marks)

29 Write the correct digit in each box.

(a)

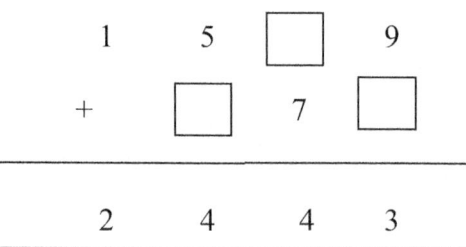

(2 marks)

$$\begin{array}{cccc} & 1 & 5 & \boxed{6} & 9 \\ + & & \boxed{8} & 7 & \boxed{4} \\ \hline & 2 & 4 & 4 & 3 \end{array}$$

29(b)

```
    ☐  6  3              5  6  3
×      ☐             ×         7
─────────────        ─────────────
 3  9  ☐  1           3  9  4  1
```

(2 marks)

30 In Miss Fryer's class, there are 5 girls for every 4 boys, and one fifth of the girls wear glasses. There are three girls and two boys in the class who wear glasses. What fraction of all the pupils in the class wear glasses?

There are three girls, who wear glasses, and one fifth of the girls wear glasses ⇒ the number of girls in the class is 15 $(= 3 \div \frac{1}{5})$.

There are 5 girls for every 4 boys ⇒ the number of boys in the class is 12 $(= \frac{15}{5} \times 4)$.

The total number of pupils is 27 in the class.

There are three girls and two boys in the class who wear glasses; it means that 5 pupils wear glasses in the class.

The fraction of all the pupils in the class wear glasses is $\frac{5}{27}$

Answer $\frac{5}{27}$ (3 marks)

Paper 3 solutions

1(a) $2\frac{1}{2}+4\frac{1}{4}$

$2\frac{1}{2}+4\frac{1}{4}=2\frac{2}{4}+4\frac{1}{4}=6\frac{3}{4}$

Answer $6\frac{3}{4}$ (1 mark)

1(b) $4\frac{1}{4}-2\frac{1}{2}$

$4\frac{1}{4}-2\frac{1}{2}=3\frac{5}{4}-2\frac{2}{4}=1\frac{3}{4}$

Answer $1\frac{3}{4}$ (1 mark)

2(a) $3\frac{1}{2}\times1\frac{1}{3}$

$3\frac{1}{2}\times1\frac{1}{3}=\frac{7}{2}\times\frac{\cancel{4}^{2}}{3}=\frac{14}{3}=4\frac{2}{3}$

Answer $4\frac{2}{3}$ (1 mark)

2(b) $10\div\frac{1}{4}$

$10\div\frac{1}{4}=10\times4=40$

Answer 40 (2 marks)

2(c) $\frac{1}{2}$ of $\frac{3}{4}$

$\frac{1}{2}\times\frac{3}{4}=\frac{3}{8}$

Answer $\frac{3}{8}$ (2 marks)

3(a) $\frac{3}{8}$ of 240 m.

$$\frac{3}{\cancel{8}_1} \times \cancel{240}^{30} = 90$$

    Answer 90 m   (2 marks)

3(b) 20% of £350

$20\% \times 350 = 0.2 \times 350 = 70$

    Answer £70   (2 marks)

4(a) £1.28+57p

£1.28+57p = £1.28+£0.57 = £1.85

    Answer £1.85   (2 marks)

4(b) £1.28−57p

£1.28−57p = 128p−57p = 71p

    Answer 71p   (2 marks)

5(a) A number is multiplied by 100 to give 2030

What is the number?

$\frac{2030}{100} = 20.3$

    Answer 20.3   (2 marks)

5(b) 7686×5

```
    3 4 3
    7 6 8 6
×         5
─────────────
    3 8 4 3 0
```

    Answer 38430   (2 marks)

Alternative method:
$$7686 \times 5 = \frac{\overset{3843}{\cancel{7686}}}{\underset{1}{\cancel{2}}} \times 10 = 3843 \times 10 = 38430$$

6(a) A Year 6 student sleeps for 9 hours every day. For what fraction of the day, in its simplest form, is the student awake?

$$\frac{24-9}{24} = \frac{15}{24} = \frac{5}{8}$$

Answer $\dfrac{5}{8}$ (2 marks)

6(b) What fraction of 2.4 litres is 400ml?

2.4 litres ÷ 6 = 400 ml

∴ $\dfrac{1}{6}$ of 2.4 litres is 400ml.

Answer $\dfrac{1}{6}$ (2 marks)

7 Write in figures the number three hundred thousand and thirty.

Answer 300030 (2 marks)

8 Put these numbers in ascending order.

$5^2 \qquad 2^5 \qquad 3^4 \qquad 4^3$

$5^2 = 25$, $2^5 = 32$, $3^4 = 81$, $4^3 = 64$

Answer $5^2 \quad 2^5 \quad 4^3 \quad 3^4$ (2 marks)

9 For a film, the seats cost £3 for each child and £8 for each adult. I was charged £52 for all the seats I bought.

9(a) Did I buy more than 6 adult tickets?

$7 \times £8 = £56 \Rightarrow £52$ can not buy more than 6 adult tickets.

Answer No (2 marks)

9(b) If there were more adult tickets than child tickets, how many of each did I buy?

Use a few trials to get the values around 52.

$6 \times 8 + 1 \times 3 = 51$, $5 \times 8 + 4 \times 3 = 52$

∴ 5 adult tickets and 4 child tickets

  Answer 5 adult tickets and 4 child tickets

             (2 marks)

9(c) If there were more child tickets than adult tickets, how many of each did I buy?

Use a similar way in part (b) to get the values around 52.

$4 \times 8 + 6 \times 3 = 50$, $3 \times 8 + 9 \times 3 = 51$, $2 \times 8 + 12 \times 3 = 52$

∴ 2 adult tickets and 12 child tickets

  Answer 2 adult tickets and 12 child tickets

             (2 marks)

10 Every day Jack runs 3 km.

10(a) Find out how far he runs in 4 weeks.

$3 \times 7 \times 4 = 84$

  Answer 84 km   (2 marks)

10(b) If he takes 15 minutes to run the 3 km, what is the average speed in kilometres per hour?

$$\frac{3 \text{ km}}{15 \text{ min}} = \frac{3 \text{ km}}{\frac{15}{60} \text{ hr}} = 12 \text{ km/hr}$$

  Answer 12 km per hour (2 marks)

11 Eggs are sold in boxes of 12, costing £1.68. I wish to make 15 cakes for a local fete. The recipe requires 5 eggs for each cake.

11(a) How many eggs will I use altogether to make 15 cakes?

$15 \times 5 = 75$

  Answer 75 eggs   (2 marks)

10

11(b) How many boxes must I buy to ensure I have enough eggs for the cakes?

$6 \times 12 = 72$, $72 < 75$

$7 \times 12 = 84$

∴ 7 boxes of eggs are needed.

        Answer   7   (2 marks)

11(c) How much will I pay for the eggs?

$7 \times £1.68 = £11.76$

        Answer   £11.76   (2 marks)

12 The exchange rate was £1 = 12 HKD.

12(a) In Hong Kong, Jack wanted buy a large bar of chocolate, which cost £3.

How much would Jack have to pay for chocolate in HKD?

$3 \times 12 = 36$

        Answer   36 HKD   (2 marks)

12(b) The price for a watch is 480 HKD.

How much is it in English pounds?

$\frac{480}{12} = 40$

        Answer   £40   (2 marks)

13 Fill in the two missing numbers in each of following sequences:

13(a) 8, 12, ☐, 20, 24, ☐, 32   (2 marks)

8, 12, 16, 20, 24, 28, 32

13(b) 256, 128, 64, ☐, 16, 8, ☐.   (2 marks)

256, 128, 64, 32, 16, 8, 4.

14   Which of the following is greater than 3 but smaller than 4?

$\dfrac{10}{3}$ $\dfrac{12}{3}$ $\dfrac{9}{3}$ $\dfrac{8}{3}$

$\dfrac{10}{3} = 3\dfrac{1}{3}$, $\dfrac{12}{3} = 4$, $\dfrac{9}{3} = 3$ and $\dfrac{8}{3} = 2\dfrac{2}{3}$

$3 < 3\dfrac{1}{3} < 4 \Rightarrow 3 < \dfrac{10}{3} < 4$

Answer $\dfrac{10}{3}$ (2 marks)

15   A pineapple costs £2.45

Jack has a £10 note.

He buys as many pineapples as he can with his £10 note.

15(a)   How many pineapples does Jack buy?

$2.45 \times 4 = 9.80$, $2.45 \times 5 = 12.25 > 10$

∴He can buy 4 pineapples by a £10 note.

Answer   4   (2 marks)

15(b)   How much change should Jack receive from his £10 note?

£10 − £9.80 = £0.20 = 20 p

Answer   20 p   (2 marks)

16   One of the angles of an isosceles triangle is 96°. Find the sizes of the other two angles.

$2 \times 96° = 192° > 180°$, thus this isosceles triangle does not have another 96° angle, and it must have the other two same angles, as follows.

$\dfrac{180° - 96°}{2} = 42°$

Answer   42°, 42°   (2 marks)

17(a) Shade in $\frac{2}{5}$ of the shape below.

(2 marks)

This shape consists of 20 small rectangles.

$20 \times \frac{2}{5} = 8$. Shade in $\frac{2}{5}$ of the shape, it means that 8 small rectangles need to be shaded as follows.

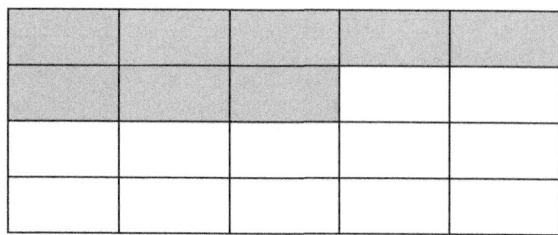

17(b) Shade in 60% of the shape below.

(2 marks)

$60\% \times 20 = 12$

In the same way mentioned in part (a). Shade in 60% of the shape, it means that 12 small rectangles need to be shaded as follows.

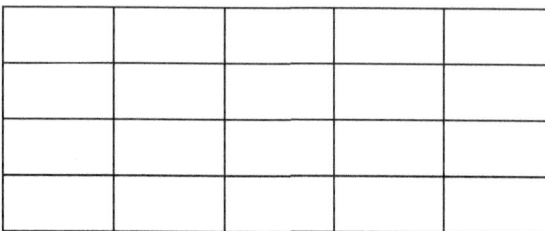

18   Emma starts with a number, doubles it and then subtracts 9. The result is 33

What number did Emma start with?

The number, which Emma started with, can be obtained by adding 9 to the result (33) and then divided by 2, as follows.

$\dfrac{9+33}{2} = 21$.

Answer   21   (2 marks)

19   Jane is $10\dfrac{1}{2}$ years old. Her brother is exactly 1 year and 8 months younger than Jane.

How old is her brother?

$10\dfrac{1}{2}$ years − 1 year 8 months = 10 years + 6 month − 1 year − 8 months

= 9 years + 18 months − 1 year − 8 months

= (9 years − 1 year) + (18 months − 8 months) = 8 years 10 months

Answer   8 years 10 months   (2 marks)

20   Here are the ingredients needed to make 12 muffins.

Ingredients to make 12 muffins
300 g flour
150 g sugar
250 ml milk
100 g butter
2 eggs

20(a)   Emma makes 60 muffins.

Work out how much flour she uses.

$\dfrac{60}{12} = 5 \Rightarrow$ She needs 5 times as much flour as she needs to make 12 muffins.

$5 \times 300\,g = 1500\,g$

Answer   1500 g   (2 marks)

6

20(b) Jack makes some muffins.

He uses 600 g sugar.

Work out how many muffins he makes.

12 muffins needs 150 g sugar

$\frac{600}{150} = 4$, which is 4 times as much as the ingredients for 12 muffins.

Thus the number of the muffins can be calculated as follows.

$4 \times 12 = 48$

Answer   48   (2 marks)

21(a) Which number between 40 and 50 is a multiple of both 4 and 6?

$4 = 2 \times 2$, $6 = 2 \times 3$.

The lowest common multiple (LCM) of 4 and 6 is:

LCM $= 2 \times 2 \times 3 = 12$

$12 \times 2 = 24$, $12 \times 3 = 36$, $12 \times 4 = 48$, $12 \times 5 = 60$. It is easy to see that 48 is the number between 40 and 50 and is also a multiple of both 4 and 6.

Answer   48   (2 marks)

21(b) Circle the three numbers in the list below which have a sum of 43.

5   8   11   14   21   31   (2 marks)

$8 + 14 + 21 = 43$

5   ⑧   11   ⑭   ㉑   31

22 Jack and Emma each think of a number.

The difference between their numbers is 8.

The sum of their numbers is 30.

What are the two numbers?

The midway of the two numbers is $\frac{30}{2} = 15$

As the difference between their numbers is 8, the smaller number is 15-4 = 11, and the bigger number is 15+4 = 19.

Answer   11, 19   (2 marks)

23 Emma has used her calculator to find out that $14 \times 541 = 7574$

Use Emma's calculator to find out

23(a) 140×541 (1 mark)

$140 \times 541 = 10 \times 14 \times 541 = 10 \times 7574 = 75740$

23(b) 14×540 (1 mark)

$14 \times 540 = 14 \times 541 - 14 = 7574 - 14 = 7560$

23(c) 24×541 (1 mark)

23(c) $24 \times 541 = 14 \times 541 + 10 \times 541 = 7574 + 5410 = 12984$

24 In the diagrams below, the square and rectangle have the same perimeter. The square has an area of 144 cm².

The length of the rectangle is three times the width of the rectangle.

Work out the length of the rectangle.

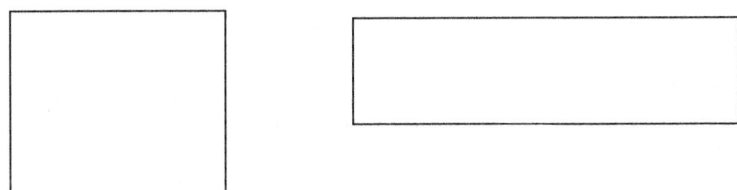

The square has an area of 144 cm², the length of a side of the square is 12 cm, the perimeter is $4 \times 12 \, \text{cm} = 48 \, \text{cm}$.

For the rectangle, $\text{length} + \text{width} = 24 \, \text{cm}$. The length of the rectangle is

$\dfrac{3}{4} \times 24 \, \text{cm} = 18 \, \text{cm}$

Answer   18 cm   (2 marks)

25 A tennis club has 240 members.

$\dfrac{1}{5}$ of the members are women.

$\dfrac{2}{5}$ of the members are men.

The rest of the members are children.

25(a) What percentage of the members are children?

$$1-\left(\dfrac{1}{5}+\dfrac{2}{5}\right)=1-\dfrac{3}{5}=\dfrac{2}{5}=0.4=40\%$$

Answer 40%   (2 marks)

25(b) How many of the members are women?

$$\dfrac{1}{5}\times 240 = 48$$

Answer 48   (2 marks)

25(c) How many of the members are men?

$$\dfrac{2}{5}\times 240 = 96$$

Answer 96   (2 marks)

26 In the diagram below (not to scale), find the angles marked x and y.

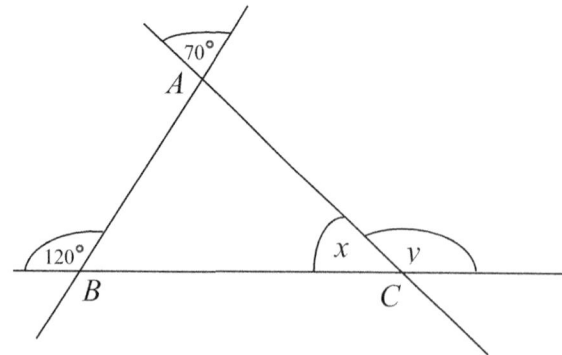

$\angle BAC = 70°$, $\angle ABC = 180° - 120° = 60°$

$x = 180° - \angle BAC - \angle ABC = 180° - 70° - 60° = 50°$

$y = 180° - x = 180° - 50° = 130°$

Answer $x = 50°$, $y = 130°$ (2 marks)

27   Draw all the lines of symmetry on each of these shapes.

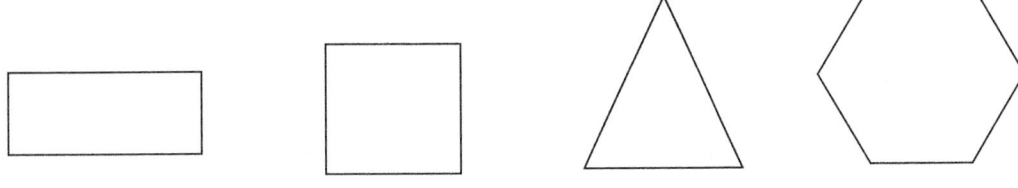

(2 marks)

All the lines of symmetry on each of these shapes are drawn with the dotted line as shown on the diagram.

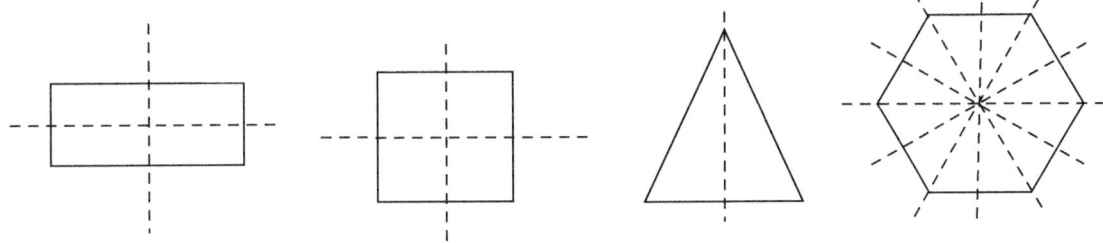

28   Draw the reflection of this triangle in the mirror line shown.

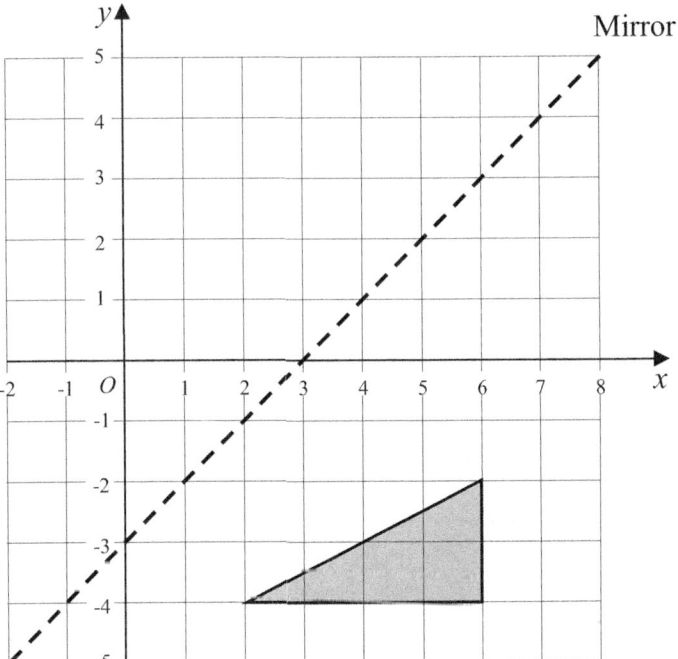

(2 marks)

The reflection of this triangle in the mirror line is drawn, triangle R, as shown on the diagram.

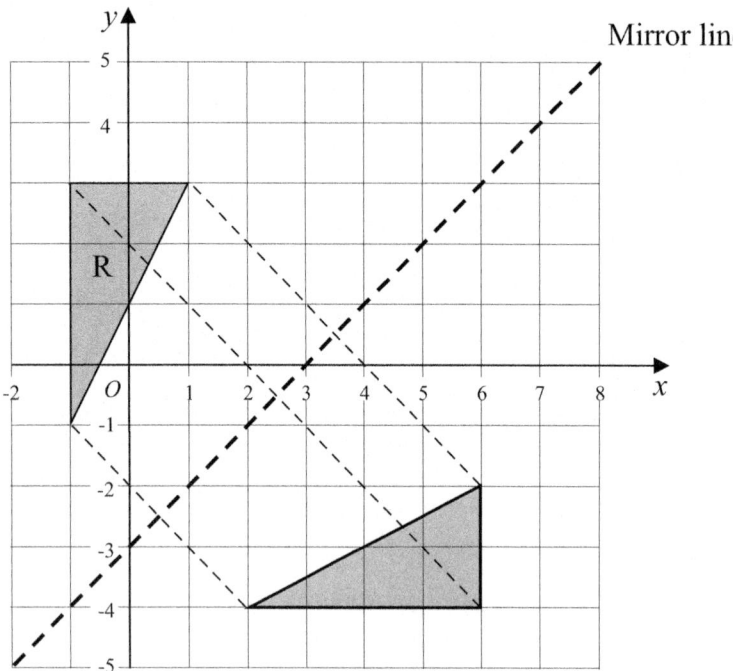

29 The four candidates in an election were A, B, C and D.

The pie chart shows the proportion of votes for each candidate.

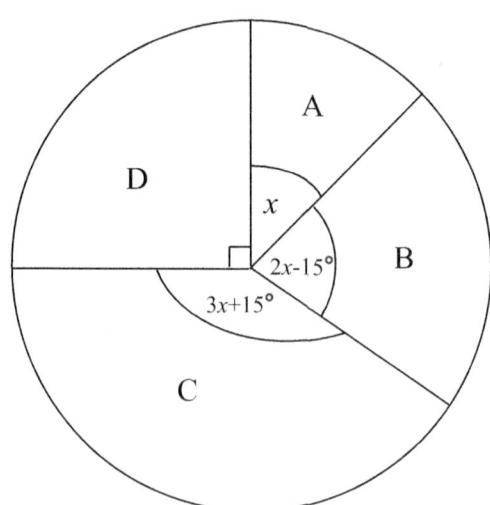

29(a) Work out the value of x

$$x + (2x - 15°) + (3x + 15°) + 90° = 360° \Rightarrow x = \frac{270°}{6} = 45°$$

Answer   45°   (2 marks)

29(b) Work out the percentage of the votes for candidate A.

$$\frac{45°}{360°} = \frac{1}{8} = 12.5\%$$

Answer   12.5%   (2 marks)

30   Can you find numbers to replace A, B and C in this sum?

(A, B and C are all different numbers)

```
      A A              8 8
      B B              9 9
  +   C C          +   1 1
  _____      _____
      C B A            1 9 8
  _____      _____
```

Answer   A = 8; B = 9; C = 1   (2 marks)

Paper 4 solutions

1. Arrange the following numbers from smallest to largest.

   $\frac{1}{3}$ 0.305   0.33 $\frac{3}{10}$

   $\frac{1}{3} = 0.33\dot{3}$, $\frac{3}{10} = 0.3$

   $\frac{3}{10}$ 0.305   0.33 $\frac{1}{3}$

   Answer $\frac{3}{10}$ 0.305   0.33 $\frac{1}{3}$

   (2 marks)

2. Put a circle around each prime number.

   3   4   5   6   7   8

   ③   4   ⑤   6   ⑦   8

   (2 marks)

3(a) Work out $\frac{1}{4}$ of 96

   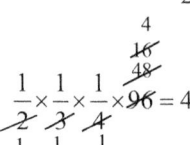

   Answer   24   (2 marks)

3(b) Work out of $\frac{1}{2}$ of $\frac{1}{3}$ of $\frac{1}{4}$ of 96

   $\frac{1}{\cancel{2}_1} \times \frac{1}{\cancel{3}_1} \times \frac{1}{\cancel{4}_1} \times \cancel{\cancel{\cancel{96}^{48}}^{16}}^{4} = 4$

   Answer   4   (2 marks)

   Note: Numerator and denominator are divided by 2, 3 and then 4.

4 Write the next two numbers in each sequence:

4(a) 100, 94, 88, 82, ... , ...

100, 94, 88, 82, 76, 70

Answer   76, 70   (2 marks)

4(b) 1, 2, 4, 7, 11, ... , ...

1, 2, 4, 7, 11, 16, 22

Answer   16, 22   (2 marks)

5 Jack is now twice his sister's age. In 5 years' time Jack will be 11. How old will his sister be then?

In 5 years' time Jack will be 11, so Jack is 6 now.

Jack is now twice his sister's age, so his sister is 3 now and will be 8 in 5 years' time.

Answer   8 years old   (3 marks)

6 The pie chart shows data collected in a survey by a PE teacher about the favourite sports of a group of school children.

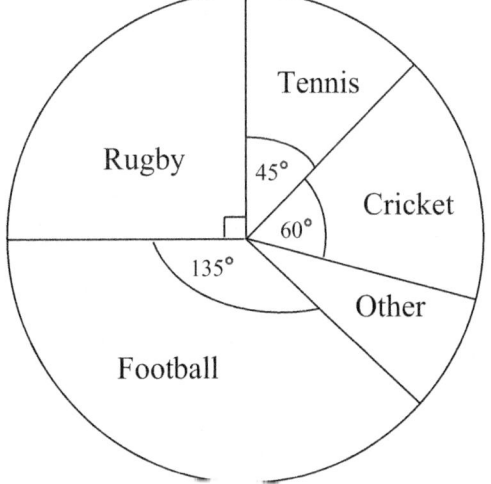

6(a) Write down the fraction of the school children who liked cricket.

Give your answer in the simplest form.

$\dfrac{60°}{360°} = \dfrac{1}{6}$

Answer $\dfrac{1}{6}$ (3 marks)

10

6(b) A total of 72 children were asked to complete the survey. Calculate how many children preferred tennis.

$$\frac{45^0}{360^0} \times 72 = 9$$

Answer   9   (3 marks)

7   Jack and Emma are on their bicycles and start 60 miles apart on a road, riding towards each other. Jack is travelling at 20 mph, while Emma is travelling at 10 mph. They set off at the same time and keep moving at constant speeds until they meet.

7(a) Work out the distance that each rider has cycled by the time they meet.

Jack's speed is twice Emma's speed.

The distance which Jack cycled is twice the distance Emma cycled in the same time.

The distance which Jack cycled is $\frac{2}{3} \times 60$ miles = 40 miles

The distance which Emma cycled is $\frac{1}{3} \times 60$ miles = 20 miles

Answer   Jack: 40 miles; Emma: 20 miles

(2 marks)

7(b) Write down the time taken for them to meet.

$$\frac{40 \text{ miles}}{20 \text{ mph}} = 2 \text{ hr}$$

Answer   2 hr   (2 marks)

8   How many tiles shaped like this: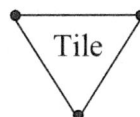

are needed to cover the figure below?

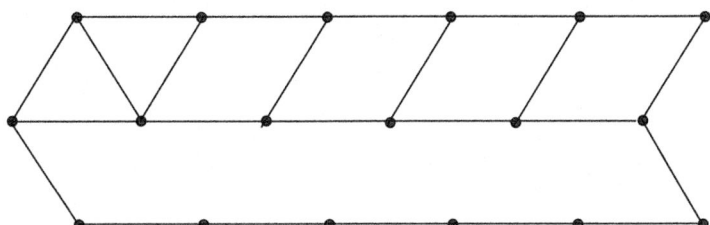

Draw the lines between the two close dots; it would be easy to calculate how many tiles are needed as follows:

$2 \times 5 \times 2 = 20$

   Answer   20   (3 marks)

9   Label each arrow with the value indicated on the scale.

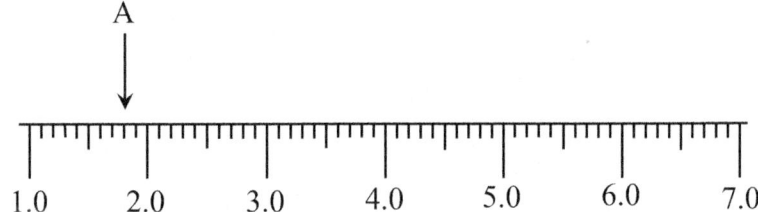

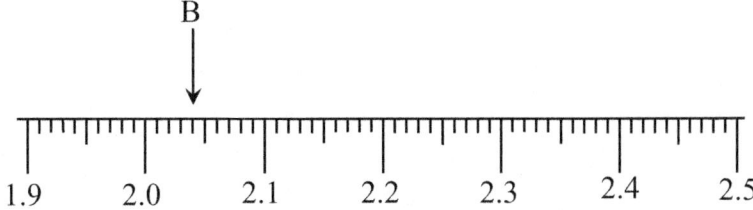

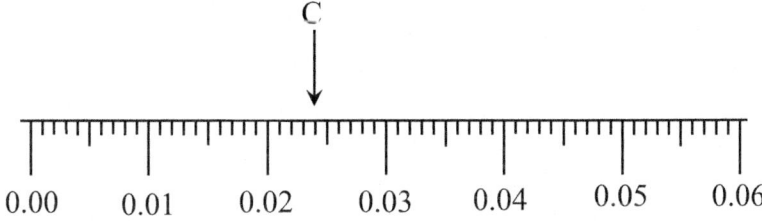

As shown on the diagrams below.

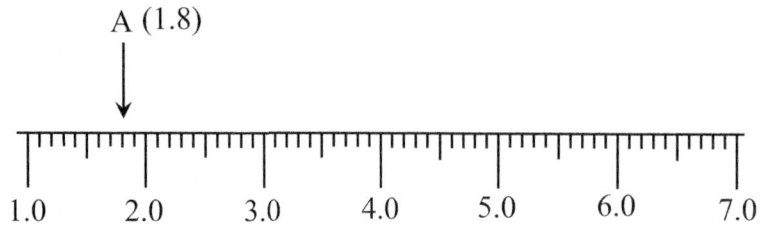

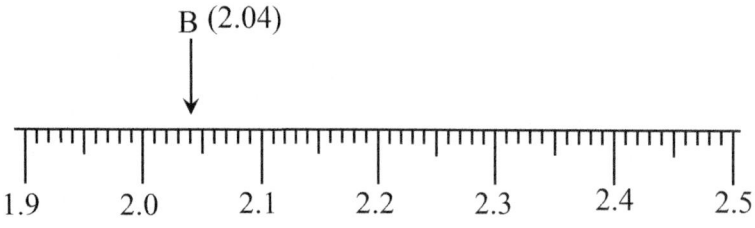

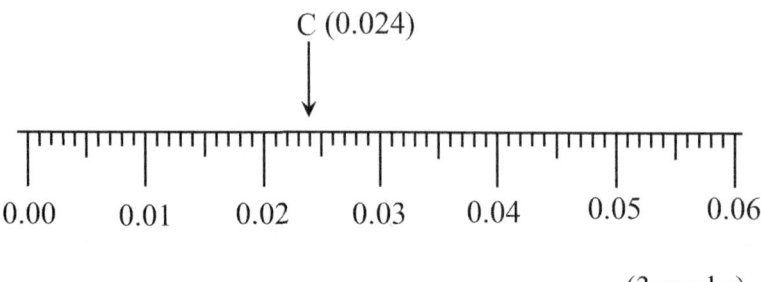

(3 marks)

10 In a class there are 30 children, the ratio of number of boys to number of girls is 3:2. Work out how many boys are in the class.

$\frac{3}{5} \times 30 = 18$

Answer   18   (3 marks)

11 A bottle of orange cordial makes enough drink to fill 40 glasses when it is diluted in the ratio 1 part cordial to 4 parts water. How many glasses of drink would a bottle of cordial make if it is diluted in the ratio 1 part cordial to 5 parts water?

$\frac{1}{5} \times 40 = 8 \Rightarrow 8$ glasses of orange cordial.

$6 \times 8 = 48 \Rightarrow 48$ glasses if it is diluted in the ratio 1 part cordial to 5 parts water.

Answer   48   (3 marks)

12   Which of these nets would fold to make a closed cube? Circle the appropriate letters.

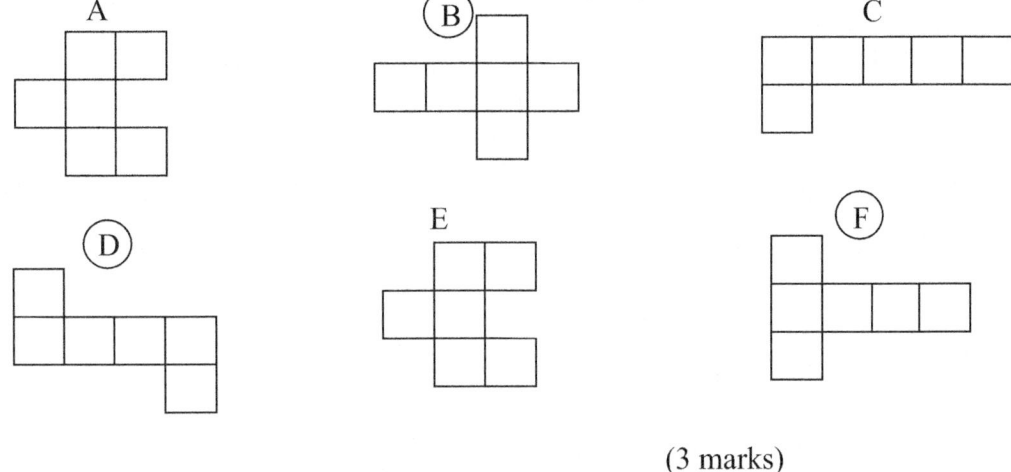

(3 marks)

13   Complete the figures below. The dotted line is the line of symmetry

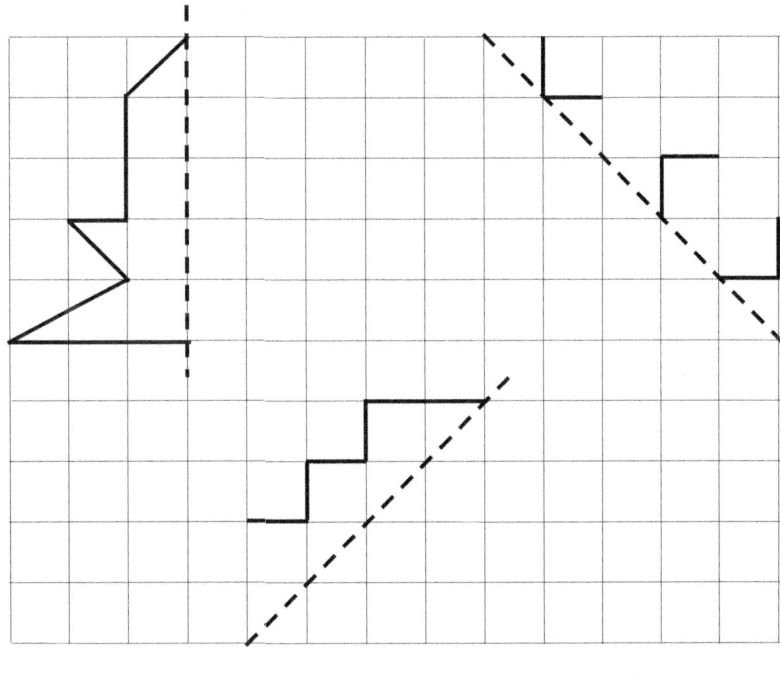

(3 marks)

Completed the figures as shown below

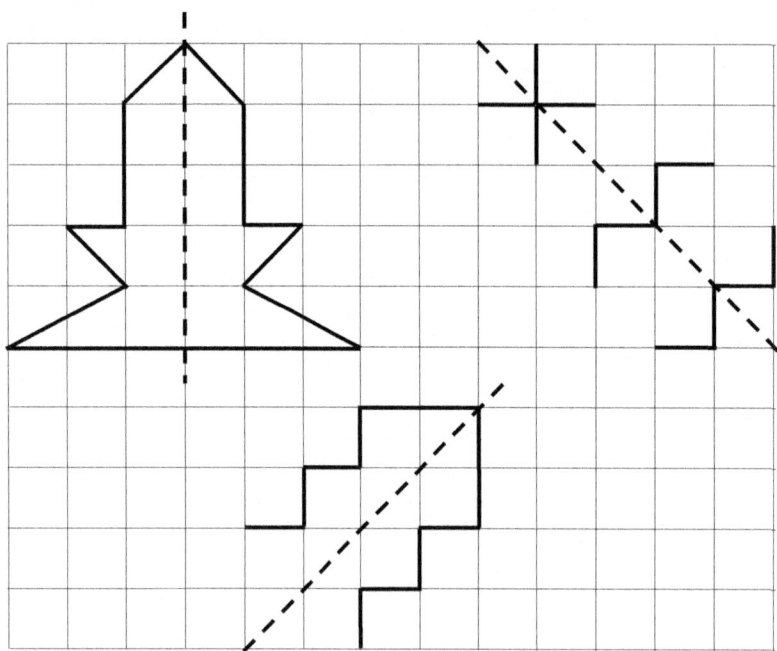

14 What is the order of rotational symmetry of these shapes?

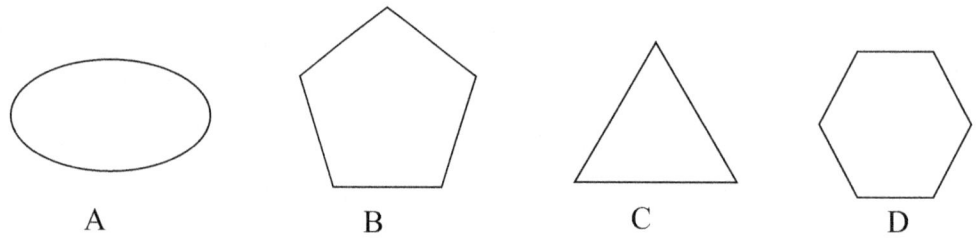

| A | B | C | D |

Answer   A: 2; B: 5; C: 3; D: 6   (2 marks)

15 Jack has 75 small wooden cubes, each measuring 1cm×1cm ×1cm. He arranges them all so that they form a cuboid. Given that the perimeter of the base of the cuboid is 16 cm, what is its height?

The perimeter of the base of the cuboid is 16cm.

length + width = 8 cm for the base.

The dimensions of the base could be 1 cm by 7 cm, 2 cm by 6 cm, 3 cm by 5 cm or 4 cm by 4 cm.

$75 = 3 \times 5 \times 5$.

Thus the dimensions of the base of the cuboid are 3 cm by 5 cm, and the height of the cuboid is 5 cm.

    Answer   5 cm   (3 marks)

16 In a group of 60 girls, each one is either blonde or brunette and is either blue-eyed or brown-eyed. 15 are blue-eyed blondes, 40 are brunettes, and 26 are brown-eyed. How many are brown-eyed brunettes?

Draw a table by the known information about the 60 girls below.

	Brown-eyed	Blue-eyed	Total
Brunette			40
Blonde		15	
Total	26		60

Then fill the remaining numbers about the 60 girls in the following order.

$60 - 40 = 20 \Rightarrow$ 20 blondes, fill "20" for blonde in the table.

$20 - 15 = 5 \Rightarrow$ 5 brown-eyed blondes, fill "5" for brown-eyed blonde in the table.

$26 - 5 = 21 \Rightarrow$ 21 brown-eyed brunettes, fill "21" for brown-eyed brunette in the table.

$40 - 21 = 19 \Rightarrow$ 19 blue-eyed blondes, fill "19" for blue-eyed blonde in the table.

$19 + 15 = 34 \Rightarrow$ 34 blue-eyed, fill "34" for blue-eyed in the table.

	Brown-eyed	Blue-eyed	Total
Brunette	21	19	40
Blonde	5	15	20
Total	26	34	60

From the table, there are 21 brown-eyed brunettes.

    Answer   21   (3 marks)

17   Here are three numbers and two operations on five cards.

   [÷]   [+]   [3]   [7]   [36]

   Arrange the cards below to give the answer 19.

   [ ] [ ] [ ] [ ] [ ] = 19

   (2 marks)

   The arrangement of the cards is shown below.

   [36]   [÷]   [3]   [+]   [7] = 19

18   A piece of cable 48 cm long is bent into the shape of a rectangle. If the length of the rectangle is 3 times its width, what is its area?

   length + width = 24 cm for the rectangle.

   length $= \dfrac{3}{4} \times 24\,\text{cm} = 18\,\text{cm}$

   width $= \dfrac{1}{4} \times 24\,\text{cm} = 6\,\text{cm}$

   Area $= 6\,\text{cm} \times 18\,\text{cm} = 108\,\text{cm}^2$

   Answer $108\,\text{cm}^2$ (3 marks)

19   The sum of the all the whole numbers from 1 to 100 inclusive is 5050. Work out the sum of the whole numbers from 2 and 101 inclusive.

   $2 + 3 + \ldots + 100 + 101 = -1 + 1 + 2 + 3 + \ldots + 100 + 101 = -1 + 5050 + 101 = 5050 + 100 = 5150$

   Answer   5150   (3 marks)

20   Jack thinks of a number.

He multiplies that number by 5. Then he subtracts 15. Then he divides by 3. Finally he adds 15. His answer is 35.

What number did Jack originally think of?

$$\frac{(35-15) \times 3 + 15}{5} = 15$$

Answer   15   (3 marks)

21   Find the value of for each of the following equations

21(a) $3x - 8 = 13$

$3x - 8 = 13 \Rightarrow 3x = 21 \Rightarrow x = 7$

Answer   7   (2 marks)

21(b) $3(2x - 5) = 21$

$3(2x - 5) = 21 \Rightarrow 2x - 5 = 7 \Rightarrow 2x = 12 \Rightarrow x = 6$

Answer   6   (2 marks)

21(c) $\frac{2x}{3} + 3 = 15$

$\frac{2x}{3} + 3 = 15 \Rightarrow \frac{2x}{3} = 12 \Rightarrow \frac{x}{3} = 6 \Rightarrow x = 18$

Answer   18   (2 marks)

22   Each square is one square unit. What is the area of the shaded hexagon?

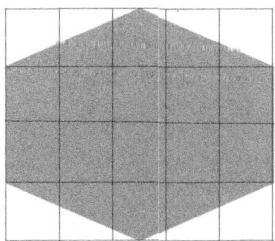

$4 \times 5 - 4 \times \frac{1 \times 2.5}{2} = 20 - 5 = 15$

Answer   15 square units   (3 marks)

23 Emma, Jack and Mark share some money. Emma gets twice as much as Jack and three times as much as Mark. If they get £44.00 in total, how much do they each get?

If Mark has 2 portions of the money, Jack would have 3 portions of the money, and Emma would have 6 portions of the money. Therefore £44.00 can be divided into 11 portions.

Mark: $\frac{2}{11} \times £44.00 = £8.00$; Jack: $\frac{3}{11} \times £44.00 = £12.00$; Emma: $\frac{6}{11} \times £44.00 = £24.00$

Answer   Mark: £8.00 ; Jack: £12.00 ; Emma: £24.00

(3 marks)

24 A ball is dropped from a height of 12 metres. It bounces off the floor to half its original height. How far will the ball have travelled when it reaches the floor for the third time?

When it reaches the floor for the first time, it has travelled: 12 metres.

When it reaches the floor for the second time, it has travelled:

12 metres + (6 meters + 6 meters).

When it reaches the floor for the third time, tt has travelled:

12 metres + (6 meters + 6 meters) + (3 meters + 3 meters) = 30 meters.

Answer   30 meters   (3 marks)

25 Consecutive numbers are one apart.

25(a) Find three consecutive numbers with a sum of 48.

The number between the smallest and biggest numbers is $\frac{48}{3} = 16$

The smallest number = 16-1 = 15

The biggest number = 16+1 = 17.

Answer   15, 16, 17   (3 marks)

25(b) Find three more consecutive numbers which give 504 when multiplied together.
(Try to find the suitable divisors of 504 step by step as follows :)

$504 = 2 \times 252 = 4 \times 126 = 8 \times 63 = 8 \times 7 \times 9$

Answer   7, 8, 9   (3 marks)

26   The scale of a map is such that 3 cm on the map represents an actual distance of 15 km.

26(a) Express the scale of the map as a ratio in the form $1:n$ where n is a whole number.

3 cm : 15 km = 3 cm : 1500000 cm = 1:500000

    Answer   1:500000   (2 marks)

26(b) The actual park is 20 km by 30 km. What are its dimensions in cm on the map?

$$\frac{20 \text{ km}}{500000} = \frac{2000000 \text{ cm}}{500000} = 4 \text{ cm}$$

$$\frac{30 \text{ km}}{500000} = \frac{3000000 \text{ cm}}{500000} = 6 \text{ cm}$$

    Answer   4 cm by 6 cm   (2 marks)

27   In a sale, normal prices were reduced by 25%

27(a) The normal price of a computer was £800

Work out the sale price of the computer.

£800 − £800 × 25% = £800 − £200 = £600

    Answer   £600   (2 marks)

27(b) The normal price of a TV was reduced by £125

Work out the normal price of the TV.

$$\frac{£125}{25\%} = £125 \times 4 = £500$$

    Answer   £500   (2 marks)

28   I got 80% on a 10-problem test, 65% on a 20-problem test and 70% on a 30-problem test.

If the three tests are combined into one 60-problem test, what percentage is my overall score?

$$\frac{10 \times 80\% + 20 \times 65\% + 30 \times 70\%}{60} = 70\%$$

    Answer   70%   (3 marks)

11

29 Jack organised a quiz night in the toy room. He asked 25 questions.

For each correct answer you gained 4 points.

For each incorrect answer you lost 2 points.

For each question you did not attempt you scored 0 points.

Emma answered all but one of the questions and got a score of 66 points.

How many correct answers did she have?

$\frac{66}{4} = 16.5 \Rightarrow$ the least possible number of correct answers is 17.

Assume that Emma got 17 correct answers, 7 incorrect answers, it would give:

$17 \times 4 - 7 \times 2 = 54$

Assume that Emma got 18 correct answers, 6 incorrect answers, it would give:

$18 \times 4 - 6 \times 2 = 60$

Assume that Emma got 19 correct answers, 5 incorrect answers, it would give:

$19 \times 4 - 5 \times 2 = 66$

Answer   19   (3 marks)

30 At a busy railway station trains leave from platform 6 every 6 minutes and from platform 8 every 8 minutes. Trains leave from both platforms at 15:57.

When do trains next leave both platforms at the same time?

$6 = 2 \times 3$, $8 = 2 \times 2 \times 2$

The lowest common multiple (LCM) of 6 and 8 is:

LCM $= 2 \times 2 \times 2 \times 3 = 24$

Therefore they will next leave together in 24 minutes.

$15\,h\,57\,min + 24\,min = 15\,h + 57\,min + 24\,min = 15\,h + 81\,min = 16\,h\,21\,min$

They will next leave together at 16:21

Answer   16:21   (3 marks)

Printed in Great Britain
by Amazon